Legends
of
Chivalry

MYTH AND MANKIND

Legends
of
Chivalry

MEDIEVAL MYTH

METRO BOOKS
NEW YORK

MYTH AND MANKIND

LEGENDS OF CHIVALRY: Medieval Myth

Writers: Tony Allan (Outlaws and Champions of Justice, Poking Fun at the Powers-that-be), Clifford
Bishop (The Medieval World; Maidens, Mysteries and Trials of Love),
Charles Phillips (The Heroes of Epic, The Legacy of Medieval Myth)
Consultant: Dr. Juliette Wood

Created, edited and designed by
Duncan Baird Publishers
Castle House
75–76 Wells Street
London W1P 3RE

Duncan Baird Publishers
Managing Editor: Diana Loxley
Managing Art Editor: Clare Thorpe
Series Editor: Christopher Westhorp
Editor: Mark McDowall
Designer: Clare Thorpe
Picture Researcher: Cecilia Weston-Baker
Commissioned Illustrations: Neil Gower
Map Artwork: Lorraine Harrison
Artwork Borders: Iona McGlashan
Editorial Researcher: Clifford Bishop

Staff for *Legends of Chivalry: Medieval Myth*
Editorial Manager: Tony Allan
Design Consultant: Mary Staples
Editorial Production: Alexia Turner

Metro Books
122 Fifth Avenue
New York, NY 10011

ISBN-13: 978-1-4351-0608-6
ISBN-10: 1-4351-0608-3

Printed and bound in China

10 9 8 7 6 5 4 3 2 1

**Title: Men being girt with swords during their investiture as knights, detail of an illustration
from an early medieval manuscript.**

**Contents page: Silver box-shaped reliquary inlaid with precious stones, from Lombardy,
late 8th century.**

Contents

THE MEDIEVAL WORLD

The one-time count of Barcelona, Ramon Berenguer II, his body racked with dysentery and the pain of unhealed wounds, lay on his cot and stared at his dented armour. His final wish was to ride out against the Muslims and die in battle, but he was too weak to rise. He was to be denied even that last shred of glory. Once suspected of fratricide, his position had meant no one could bring him to justice. Only when he lost a battle to El Cid during Spain's Christian-Muslim civil wars did he became vulnerable enough to prosecute.

It was believed the outcome of a trial by combat would determine Berenguer's guilt, because God would not allow an innocent man to be defeated. He lost, and to escape punishment volunteered to go on the First Crusade. Secretly he had hoped that he would be able to conquer some lands for himself. Instead he had encountered only sickness, defeat and death.

Berenguer's story is not untypical of medieval nobles. Inspired by the tales of warrior heroes like Alexander the Great and Charlemagne, such men considered themselves to be soldiers for a cause, aiming to rebuild the glories of the Roman Empire. They swore loyalty to the Church and tried to live by exalted codes of knightly conduct, although family feuds and assassinations were rife as members fought over the spoils they accumulated.

Their ability to serve depended on their strength of arms, yet the very expense of being a knight often caused men to lapse from the expected standard of behaviour. Holy wars became an excuse for pillage, and murderous campaigns were waged that disfigured Europe even as they passed into folklore. Driven by legends, such men aspired to impossible ideals.

The term "Middle Ages" was introduced by Renaissance humanists inspired by a mission to revive the learning and culture of the ancient Greek and Roman worlds. The notion of a millennium-long "dark age" of ignorance took root, but like Berenguer the scholars had confused myth and reality. In declaring themselves the inheritors of the classical past, they had overlooked the medieval foundations upon which they themselves were building. For out of the turmoil of Rome's collapse had already risen a civilization with new structures, philosophies and art forms: the medieval world of Western Christendom, the immediate ancestor of Renaissance Europe.

Opposite: **Bodiam Castle, in East Sussex, England. Almost continuous hostilities meant that medieval nobles built themselves fortified houses or castles, mostly of masonry, from the 11th century onwards.**

Below: **Bishop's mitre with a gold and silk embroidered image of the coronation of the Virgin Mary, French, 14th century. The Christian Church provided a spiritual and moral focus for people in the Middle Ages.**

A Roman Inheritance

In AD364 Emperor Valentinian officially divided the Roman Empire in two. Despite the portents, the Eastern or Byzantine Empire survived and flourished until its fortress capital, Constantinople, fell to the Ottomans in 1453. The Western Roman Empire, by contrast, collapsed and a new power was born – Western Christendom, which fused the ancient customs of the Mediterranean lands with those of the northern European peoples.

By the onset of the fifth century AD, the Roman Empire was in terminal decay. Destabilized for some time by waves of "barbarian" invaders, the Roman administration was becoming dependent for its survival on sowing discord within the ranks of the forces ostensibly ranged against it – a mix of tribes, with the Germanic Visigoths, Ostrogoths and Vandals and the Asiatic Huns most dominant. Fragile alliances were forged and broken repeatedly among the mutually antagonistic parties, but the die was cast. The Eternal City, unharmed for nearly a millennium, was to be sacked three times in the space of just half a century.

The Rise of the Germanic Peoples

At Adrianople in 378 the legions were defeated by Visigoth cavalry; the warrior on horseback was in the ascendant. By this time, however, even the Roman army was composed mainly of so-called "barbarians" – in reality, cultivated but warlike peoples eager to fill any power vacuum. Germanic peoples had begun to settle in most of the western Mediterranean, posing a threat but not yet interfering in the Roman administration.

The death of Attila the Hun in 453 dispirited his people and boosted the confidence of the Germanic tribes, who had always feared the Huns. In 476 Odovacar led an army which deposed the boy-emperor Romulus and formally ended the Western Roman Empire. Its demise may be said to mark the birth of medieval Europe.

Odovacar was anxious to observe the patterns of "civilized" Roman behaviour. Elsewhere in Europe, too, the barbarian kings, with the exception of the Vandals and the Anglo-Saxons, were happy to receive imperial honours in return for empty vows of obedience. But while Odovacar respected Roman achievements, he did little to preserve them, and the eastern emperor succeeded in persuading the Ostrogoth leader Theodoric to overthrow him in an attempt to restore Rome to its former glory. Theodoric was the first barbarian king to make his own people, the Goths, as well as the Romans, subject to Roman law.

But power and influence were moving inexorably away from their traditional Mediterranean homeland. By the late fifth century the barbarian forces were coalescing into kingdoms and territorial entities, influenced by Roman traditions and culture. The Vandals had spread across North Africa and the Mediterranean islands; the Visigoths across Iberia and the territories of Aquitania (most of modern France); the Ostrogoths across Italy and the Adriatic; the Burgundians throughout the Alpine regions; and the Franks across northern parts of what are now France and Germany.

A 6th-century mosaic of the emperor Justinian (reigned 527–565) flanked by members of his court with Archbishop Maximian and General Belisarius at his sides. Justinian was responsible for a revival of Byzantine fortunes.

While secular political power ebbed north-wards, religion provided one of the strongest links to the past. The supremacy of Latin (and the Romance languages which grew from it) was one token of continuity. By 1300 a new and radically transformed Europe would emerge, rooted in northwest Europe, as the centre of a new civiliza-tion and the precursor to the modern world.

The Roman Catholic Church

Ironically, the man who did most to decimate Italy in the sixth century was not a barbarian, but the Byzantine ruler Justinian. Spurred by the dream of

reuniting the old Roman Empire, he repeatedly invaded the country, only to be driven out again by different barbarian groups. His goal was not simply to recapture lost ground; he also saw him-self rescuing the Catholics from the rule of Arian heretics (see box, page 11), and setting up a uni-versal state modelled on God's heavenly city.

One of the defining aspects of the entire, 1,000-year-long medieval period was the rise to greatness of the Roman Catholic Church. Partly shaped by the aspirations of Justinian, the Church offered a replacement for many of the institutions which had crumbled with the Western Roman Empire. For at this time it was the only body able

to impose some form of unity on a multilingual, multicultural, socially fragmented jumble of kingdoms and territories across the breadth of Europe.

Church and state had been entwined since the earlier conversion to Christianity of the Roman emperor Constantine during the fourth century. Constantine had begun the practice of convening general councils to decide a unified Church policy and these were generally held in the metropolis, or capital city, of a province. It was natural for the bishop of that place to preside, so metropolitan bishops began to acquire extra power and seniority. Gradually the hierarchy of the Church started to organize itself along similar lines to the erstwhile imperial administration.

Gregory the Great

It was Pope Gregory the Great, at the end of the sixth century, who took the first steps towards organizing a papal state and subjugating all the bishops to papal rule. When he became pope, the Germanic Lombards led by King Alboin had invaded Italy and reduced the imperial forces to a narrow strip of land between Rome in the west and Ravenna in the east. However, despite the barbarian threat, the wealth of the Church was growing. Landowners who could not pay their taxes would often surrender their property to the local bishop, and many rich men were entering the Church and bringing their estates with them.

Gregory found himself acting as a temporal as well as spiritual ruler. He advanced money to pay the imperial troops and appointed military commanders of his own to defend Rome. He also began to assert his political independence, coming into conflict with the emperor by deciding, unilaterally, to make peace with the Lombards. Gregory was a realist and knew that the best chance for the Church's survival was not to fight the barbarians, but to convert them. His vision was borne out, for over the following centuries the Church became an increasingly strong centralized power under the firm control of Rome.

Pope Gregory the Great leads a procession to end an outbreak of the plague in Rome, from the Limbourg brothers' *Tres Riches Heures du Duc de Berry*, early 15th century. Gregory was instrumental in establishing the primacy of papal rule in Western Christendom.

Barbarian Defenders of Rome

The term "barbarian" was purely a legal definition, applied by the Romans to anyone foreign who lived outside the empire. From the third century on there was an influx of these aliens; many were refugees, and were welcomed as possible defenders of Rome.

The invaders who crossed the empire's borders in the fourth and fifth centuries AD were Germanic peoples, who were fleeing from the Mongol Huns. Beginning with the Visigoths, they requested asylum and the right to settle, and the emperor had little choice but to agree. Officially, the barbarians became *federati*, or allies of the Roman Empire. They agreed to fight for the emperor in return for board and lodging on Roman estates, or, later, for portions of the estates themselves.

The Western Germans – the Franks, Angles and Saxons – had already developed their own agricultural way of life, while the Eastern Germans – including the Goths, Vandals, Burgundians and Lombards – were nomadic.

These tribes shared a social structure based around kin-groups, or extended families.

The Goths, Vandals and Burgundians were already Christian, although they were Arians who believed that Jesus was younger and less divine than God. The Catholic Church had declared the idea heretical, and it provided a source of tension with Rome that eventually resulted in conflict.

A threat was posed to both Rome and the Germanic peoples by the Magyars, fierce horsemen who had migrated from western Siberia and first appeared in the West as mercenaries fighting for the Frankish kings, (see pages 16–18).

They were crushed decisively by the Germanic king, Otto the Great, at Lechfeld in 955. This victory was compared to the Frankish defeat of the Muslims in 732. It allowed Otto to unify his squabbling German duchies in one great cause, gained him a reputation as the saviour of Christendom and paved the way for him to become the Holy Roman Emperor.

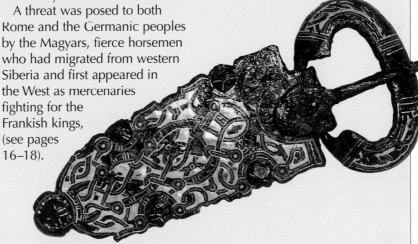

A Merovingian buckle made from iron inlaid with silver, c.AD600, a piece reflective of the dynasty's high culture.

Charlemagne, Holy Roman Emperor

The champions of Christendom in Europe were the Frankish kingdoms. Coming to the fore under Clovis in the fifth century, the Franks were later instrumental in repelling the advance of Arab forces into France in 732. But this line of kings reached its high point with the crowning of Charles, a king who earned the title "the Great", becoming known to history as Charlemagne.

Charlemagne saw it as his duty to defend all Christendom "against the attacks of pagan infidels from without" and to "fortify it from within with knowledge of the Catholic faith". Personally identified with a militant Catholicism, Charlemagne fought against all the hostile tribes of Europe, and in the process enlarged his kingdom until it covered the whole of modern France, Belgium, Holland and Switzerland, along with most of western Germany, large territories in Italy and parts of northern Spain – almost the entire Roman Catholic world.

Charlemagne also imported scholars into Gaul from all parts of his kingdom in an effort to revive culture and learning, and passed a law that reading and writing should be taught in Frankish monasteries and churches so that the clergy would be "chaste in the lives they led, but also scholars in the language that they spoke". His court became the stuff of legend, and every subsequent French or German king would hark back to compare himself to Charlemagne. Tales of his greatness and his retinue of followers, particularly the paladins, were repeated inspirationally for centuries.

While Christian missionaries went peaceably about their work in Europe, the Franks favoured more direct action, waging a brutal campaign against the pagan Frisians and Saxons. In 772, the sacred pagan tree, Irminsul, was cut down, and baptism was made compulsory as a declaration of loyalty to the invaders. Later, in 785, Charlemagne ordered the death penalty for Saxons who refused baptism, or insulted Christianity in any way.

Anglo-Saxon missionaries, who had linguistic and cultural ties to the conquered people, were regarded as useful allies by the Franks. At the same time they were able to begin reorganizing the Frankish Church according to the pattern devised by Gregory. A powerful, centralized papal state was established, owning lands and wielding power throughout large parts of Europe.

However, the strength of its protector, the emperor, was always perceived by the papacy as at best a necessary evil and at worst a threat. In 773 Pope Hadrian I begged Charlemagne to save Rome from the onslaught of the Lombards, but the victorious monarch was snubbed by not being allowed to spend a single night in the city. When Hadrian's successor, Pope Leo III, was accused of perjury and adultery, and deposed by conspirators, Charlemagne marched on Rome and summoned a general synod which allowed Leo to swear an oath "proving" his innocence. Two days later, on Christmas Day AD800, Leo gratefully crowned Charlemagne as Emperor of the Romans. In Charlemagne's eyes, the pope was simply recognizing him for what he already was. The pope, however, thought that he was conferring an honour and asserting his own superiority.

The tension between Church and state continued throughout the lifetime of the Holy Roman Empire. Yet it was precisely Charlemagne's links with Christianity that helped him become a model of chivalric honour when the writers of the twelfth and thirteenth centuries looked back to the Carolingian age for models of heroism.

Charlemagne on his throne, from the *Psalter of Charles the Bold*, c.15th century. As the first Christian emperor of the West, Charlemagne was lauded for ridding the continent of barbarism.

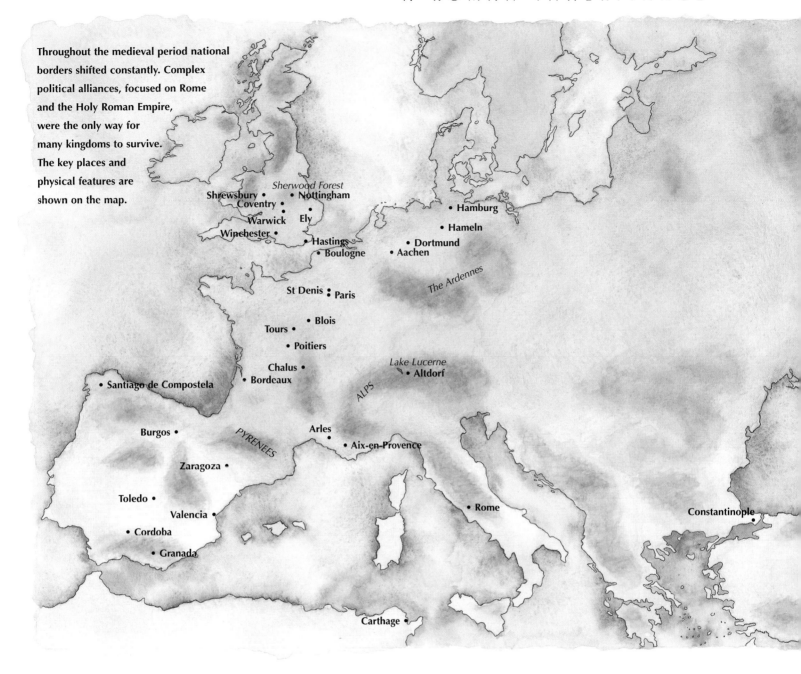

Throughout the medieval period national borders shifted constantly. Complex political alliances, focused on Rome and the Holy Roman Empire, were the only way for many kingdoms to survive. The key places and physical features are shown on the map.

Sherwood Forest

Shrewsbury • • Nottingham
Coventry •
Warwick • Ely
Winchester • • Hastings
• Boulogne

• Hamburg
• Hameln
• Dortmund
• Aachen

The Ardennes

St Denis • Paris

• Blois
Tours •
• Poitiers

Lake Lucerne
Chalus • • Altdorf
• Bordeaux

ALPS

• Santiago de Compostela

Burgos • Arles •
• Aix-en-Provence

PYRENEES

Zaragoza •

Toledo •

Valencia • • Rome

Cordoba • Constantinople •

• Granada

Carthage •

The Rise of Islam

Whatever the internal, political rivalries of the former territories of the Western Roman Empire, the force which eventually served to bind together the nascent nations of Europe – albeit only on occasions – was the Christian religion. At the beginning, however, Christianity itself was not a united doctrine and paganism remained deeply entrenched in many areas. When a new, rival religion emerged in the east in the form of Islam, it posed a serious challenge.

A faith of the Near East and North Africa, Islam too drew on earlier traditions – including the cultures of Mesopotamia and Persia – to forge a new and powerful civilization. The founder of Islam, Mohammed, was born in Mecca around AD570. He was forty years old when he declared that he had been called by God to be a prophet, but after twelve years preaching unsuccessfully in his polytheistic home city, he moved north to Medina, where he already had a band of ex-Jewish converts. This journey is known as the *hejira*,

13

Caravan going to Mecca, from the *Maqamat*, illustrated by Hariri, late 13th century. The rise of Islam was to have a profound impact on western Europe – not only in terms of trade and learning but also as a formidable military challenge.

at Antioch, Alexandria and Jerusalem, had fallen into Muslim hands, and for the first time in centuries Constantinople itself seemed to be in greater danger than Rome.

The Muslims were helped in these conquests by Christian divisions. Although Christianity was perceived as the binding agent of the Byzantine Empire, and although its peoples were all nominally Christian, many of them were, in the eyes of the emperor and the eastern Orthodox Church, outcasts and heretics. Most Egyptians, for example, belonged to the Coptic Church; they were Monophysites, who believed that the divine nature of Christ had absorbed his humanity – and as such were persecuted ruthlessly by the powerful elite of the Melkite (or King's) Church. As a consequence, Coptics had less reason to hate the Muslims than they did the Christian Byzantine emperor.

In contrast, Islam gradually became more tolerant. In 661, leadership passed from the companions and family of Mohammed to the Umayyads, an aristocratic Arab family who ruled from Damascus. They made no attempt to convert their conquered subjects, preferring to turn a profit by taxing unbelievers instead. In return they did not confiscate property, and guaranteed freedom of worship so long as there was no attempt to convert any Muslims and the Cross was not displayed in public. Within 100 years of Mohammed's death, Islam had conquered the Persian Empire as far east as India, and Muslim rulers controlled large parts of the North African coastline and Spain. Yet despite prolonged sieges, Constantinople survived, successfully defending most of what is now Turkey. In the west the Muslims were finally checked in 732 at Poitiers, in what is considered to be one of the turning points in world history.

which means "breaking of ties", because it was in Medina that Mohammed decided he would have to convert his own people by force.

Mohammed died in 632, just two years after riding in triumph into Mecca. After only two more years, the Muslims, as Islam's followers were known, had conquered almost all of Arabia, and begun incursions into Palestine and Syria. The speed of their advance was astonishing and a source of terror to the Byzantine Empire and the Christian Church. Soon, three of the most important eastern patriarchates, or metropolitan centres,

The Spanish Cauldron

The Muslim Arabs had invaded Spain in 711, when Tarik landed at Algeciras with 7,000 men and crushed the Visigoth army. Many nobles converted to Islam and the Arabs then moved steadily north, crossing the Pyrenees. By 725 they had taken Arles and Toulouse in modern-day France.

Odo, Duke of Aquitaine, was driven back north of Bordeaux, and it looked as if the whole of Gaul was defenceless. In the northeast, however, Charles Martel had been building up a powerful cavalry, funded by lands that he had confiscated from the Church. The army of loyal knights that he established not only stopped the Muslim advance, but also had a profound influence on the development of medieval culture. The Franks had occasionally used cavalry before, but this was the first time that a major victory by an avowedly Christian army was credited to men on horseback.

Mounts and armour were expensive. Only nobles could afford the cost, and they could meet the expense solely by virtue of lands granted to them by the king, to whom they swore fealty (see pages 22–23). Although the age of chivalry – with its ideal of the disciplined warrior, courageous in battle, loyal to his king and his lady, and fighting in the service of God – was still several hundred years away, it was a direct product of the rise of the cavalry as the spearhead of medieval warfare.

Despite the defeat at Poitiers, the Muslims were not finally driven back across the Pyrenees until 759, eighteen years after Charles's death. Subsequent attacks by Charles's grandson Charlemagne, pockets of Christian resistance and internal disputes among the Islamic nobility could not free Spain from Muslim rule, where, in the major cities, a Mozarabic culture flourished among those Christians living under Islam but not converting. However, the country was no longer an Islamic emirate. In 750 the Umayyads were overthrown and killed by the Abbasids, who declared themselves the new leaders of Islam. From Baghdad, they began to run the empire as an opulent, oriental monarchy. They were also less tolerant of other religions, and placed an emphasis on converting the conquered. Most medieval descriptions of Islamic wealth, cruelty and decadence are – however loosely – based on the Abbasid caliphate.

One Umayyad prince, Abd-ar-Rahman, escaped the slaughter of his family and fled to Spain, which he declared an independent state. The descendants of Abd-ar-Rahman I were powerful rulers, and it was not until the beginning of the eleventh century that the Moorish government began to weaken and fragment into groups of squabbling *taifa*, or "party kings". The two major Christian strongholds in Spain – centred on Castile and Leon in the northwest, and Navarre and Aragon in the east – began to exploit the situation by extorting tribute in return for protection and military assistance. Spain was a Christian frontier territory – the northeastern lands of the Berenguers in the Spanish March particularly so – where raiders could make themselves fortunes and social castes were fluid. By military prowess, low-born men could aspire to the rank of noblemen, and heroes such as El Cid (see pages 48–55) could rise from nowhere to greatness. Piecemeal expansion of Christian-held lands acquired a focus and momentum which was largely the haphazard work of such opportunists, who were attracted from across Europe.

Following the capture of Toledo in 1085, King Alfonso VI of Castile converted the mosque into a cathedral. From that point

Fighting animals adorn an ivory casket that once belonged to Al Mughira, the son of Abd-ar-Rahman III, Umayyad emir of Cordoba, c.968.

onwards the Christians became less tolerant of the reconquered Muslims. Allied armies coming across the Pyrenees into the Spanish March increasingly pressed the Spanish rulers to consider themselves as vassals of the pope, engaged in a crusade of reconquest, *La Reconquista*. By the mid-thirteenth century most of the peninsula had been retaken and even Cordoba in the south had fallen. Only the Kingdom of Granada remained unconquered until 1492, when a long-swelling wave of intolerance culminated in the expulsion of both Jews and Muslims from Spain.

A New Germanic Empire

In central Europe Charlemagne's empire was torn apart after his death in 814 by civil war between his grandchildren, and although one of them, Lothar, continued to call himself emperor, it was largely an empty title. Of the Frankish lands, the west became kingdoms which went to make up France, the east Germany. The centre – from the Netherlands to Italy – crumbled into smaller states influenced by their larger neighbours.

At the same time, Europe, having averted a Muslim invasion, was subjected to new waves of incursions, from the Viking seamen to the north and the Magyar horsemen in the east. Prior to Carolingian times the Vikings were familiar as traders, but by 790 Charlemagne was organizing coastal defences against their pirate raids. For the next 200 years they terrorized the monasteries and towns of northern Europe, especially those near the sea or on navigable rivers.

In 911 King Charles the Simple bribed the Viking leader Rollo to call off his attacks by giving him Rouen and its surrounding countryside. In less than 100 years Rollo's descendants had expanded this base into the independent duchy of Normandy (from "North Men", a term for the Vikings). By this time England had a powerful, unified kingdom, both orderly and civilized. It was to undergo invasion and defeat in 1066 by these same Normans, thereby cementing its relationship with mainland Europe. A feudal society was then imposed, often

brutally, upon the English, creating much ill-will. This in turn fuelled popular tales of resisting heroes, among which the most widely known are those about Robin Hood (see pages 106–109).

For their part, within a century the Normans had also acquired – through marriage and annexation – Anjou, Poitou and Aquitaine. Their Angevin Empire for a while rivalled the realm of the French monarch until King Philip II Augustus reconquered all except Aquitaine in 1204–14. They were among the most enlightened patrons of the age of chivalry, and some of the most famous medieval stories and romances were composed at their courts.

The Magyars first appeared in the West as mercenaries fighting for the Frankish kings, before deciding to form raiding parties of their own. They too terrorized Europe until they were crushed

The Great Centres of Learning

Monasteries and cathedral schools preserved theological knowledge, but as early as the ninth century there was a call for educational centres that went further, into the fields of medicine, philosophy and law. No one anticipated how much these new universities would depend on non-Christian scholarship.

There was a medical school at Salerno from the ninth century, and a school of law at Bologna from about 1000, but it was the University of Paris which revolutionized education. It arose in the twelfth century when the cathedral schools of Notre Dame and the Ile de la Cite began to attract scholars who, rather than entering the cathedrals' service, preferred to take fee-paying students. The university was an ecclesiastical institution but these teachers would often challenge the orthodoxy of the Church.

The greatest intellectual revolution of all, however, occurred when Arab texts – often translated by Jews – began to be taught in the universities. And it was in Spain where this practice flourished, a beneficial by-product of the centuries-long Muslim occupation.

The arts and sciences of the Orient were highly advanced. They entered the West via great centres of learning and education in places such as Toledo and Cordoba.

One of the most influential was the School of Translators in Toledo – Spain's capital in the twelfth century – established by Alfonso X. Toledo remained a meeting place for Arab, Christian and Jewish cultures in spite of *La Reconquista*, and this fusion helped to spread an awareness of mathematical and scientific works such as those of the Muslim scholar Averroes. The Arabs had preserved and expanded the work of the classical Greek philosophers, who were largely forgotten in the West. Under their influence, the intellectual discipline of scholasticism flourished. Writers such as Thomas Aquinas helped to establish Aristotle as one of the most influential thinkers in Christendom, in place of the Church Father St Augustine. Philosophers thus began to speculate on the natural order of the universe without automatically attributing everything to the will of God.

The Mezquita in Cordoba, which dates from the late 8th century, remains the finest example of high Islamic architecture in Europe and is still one of the world's largest mosques. The ancient, Andalusian city was the capital of the Umayyad dynasty.

The Heroes of the Three Matters

The writers of the twelfth and thirteenth centuries were hungry for tales of adventure, magic and heroism that they could retell and make their own. They did not care where they found their stories, but there were three particularly fertile sources.

The romance was a story in prose or poetry that superseded the older, epic *chanson de geste*, or "song of great deeds". Romances were written in the vernacular (this is the original

meaning of the Old French word, *romanz*) rather than in Latin and enjoyed their heyday from the mid-twelfth to the thirteenth centuries. The writer Jean Bodel (1167–1210) claimed that romances could be divided into three great story-telling traditions, or matters: those of Rome, France and Britain.

Some of the earliest romances were based on tales from antiquity, such as the *Roman d'Eneas*, which was inspired by Virgil. The deeds of Alexander the Great

Scenes from the *Histoire de Merlin* which dealt with a central figure in the Matter of Britain, 13th century.

had generated many legends, and these were very popular in the twelfth century, finding their way into the *Roman d'Alexandre* and the later *King Alisaunder*. All these classically derived stories are grouped as the Matter of Rome.

The adventures of Charlemagne and his knights, such as Roland and Ferumbras, comprised the Matter of France. Those stories were closely related to the *chansons de geste*.

The Matter of Britain was a highly influential Celtic cycle of tales about King Arthur and his knights. Many were recorded in the 1130s in Geoffrey of Monmouth's *History of the Kings of Britain* and *Prophecies of Merlin*. They were made popular from the late eleventh century by Breton minstrels and French and German authors such as Chretien de Troyes and Wolfram von Eschenbach.

decisively by the Germanic king, Otto the Great, at Lechfeld in 955. This victory allowed Otto to unify his squabbling duchies in one great cause, gained him a reputation as the saviour of Christendom and paved the way for him to become the new Holy Roman Emperor, rivalling the Byzantine rulers. For their part, the Magyars settled in Hungary where they remain to this day.

Otto's chance came in much the same way as Charlemagne's, when he marched on Rome to rescue Pope John XII in 961. Almost as soon as Otto left Rome, the pope started forming alliances with

his enemies. Otto summoned a council of bishops to depose John, accusing him of treason and many other crimes, and installed one of his own followers in John's place. In future the emperor was to be the ruler of Christianity, and the pope his lieutenant. The Romans fought back and elected their own pope, but Otto once more deposed him. At the time of his death Otto's authority was complete, but the resentment of the Roman clergy survived him along with his empire, newly established on the principle of indivisible kingship to maintain its size and strength.

The Papacy Resurgent

When Emperor Henry III died in 1056, leaving his six-year-old son to succeed him, the churchmen attempted to break free. The Romans seized the opportunity to elect a pope without the ruler's permission, and an era of reform began which was to make the papacy the greatest power in Europe.

In 1059 Pope Nicholas II decreed that the pope should no longer be chosen by the people, the clergy of Rome, nor even by the emperor, but by a convention of the cardinal bishops. He then began to bolster this new assertion of independence by making defensive alliances with enemies of the emperor, especially the king of France and the Norman rulers of Sicily. The Normans had been invited to Sicily as Lombard mercenaries in 1016, but had turned against their employers. Although they were little more than warriors and pirates, Pope Nicholas II signed a treaty with them and offered to make their leader, Robert Guiscard, the duke of Calabria and Apulia if he agreed to become the Church's protector in the region. Since the Holy Roman Emperor claimed all the lands of Italy as his, this was as good as a declaration of war, and from that moment the Normans were instrumental in keeping the Holy Roman Empire out of southern Italy.

It was Pope Gregory VII, nearly twenty years later, who made the most sweeping changes to the clergy. In addition to laws aimed at enforcing the celibacy of priests (which meant that kings tolerated bishop's landholdings because no heirs existed, leaving them in the gift of the monarch), he declared among other things that the pope could not be judged by anyone and that he had the power to depose emperors. In 1076 he excommunicated and deposed Henry IV, throwing the whole of Europe into a state of civil war between the followers of the emperor and those of the Church.

Henry IV responded by appointing his own pope, invading Rome and having himself recrowned, but he had already lost the religious authority that had once attached itself to the office of king. From now on the pope – elected by the cardinals – was the leader of the Christian world. Although later emperors, such as Frederick I Barbarossa (1152–90), tried to restore the imperial grandeur in Italy, they were hampered by the strength of the trade-rich Lombard cities, the military might of the Sicilian Normans and the festering internal divisions in Germany. Even Barbarossa's grandson Frederick II, who was the heir to both the Holy Roman Empire and Sicily, was eventually broken by the forces of the Church.

By 1200, however, although the cities of Italy were stirring, the European balance of power had begun to move west once again. Paris had become a great capital city of culture, with no equivalent in Germany. Law was now one of the favoured subjects in the new hothouses of learning.

The imperial crown of Otto the Great (912–973), from whose imposing shadow the papacy emerged during the 11th century.

The Crusades for the Holy Land

Although Pope Eugenius III had declared the recovery of Spain to be a full crusade, the Church's most coveted prize had always been Jerusalem, held by various Muslim nationalities often collectively referred to as "Saracens". The first crusade was called by Pope Urban II in 1095. He announced absolution in advance for any sins committed by those who took part, and ordered that the Christian armies should set out on the Day of Assumption the following year.

When the crusaders duly arrived at Constantinople, the Byzantine emperor was horrified by their numbers and the potential threat they posed to his realm. He refused to let them cross the Bosphorus until they had sworn an oath of fealty, and would not have admitted them at all except for the fact that he had already suffered a string of setbacks at the hands of the Croats, the Serbs, the Normans and the Turks.

The crusaders fought their way through Asia Minor, overcoming both disease and resistance to capture Antioch. Their conquest of Jerusalem in 1099, however, owed as much to luck as to their

bravery. The Turks were otherwise engaged fighting the Mamluk Egyptians in Palestine, so the crusaders met no unified resistance and massacred the city's inhabitants. The Church had intended to make Jerusalem part of the Holy See, but the papal legate had died at Antioch, so the crusaders elected Godfrey de Bouillon as their ruler. When he died the following year, his brother Baldwin declared himself king.

Most crusaders returned home after the capture of Jerusalem, so Baldwin had to defend the annexed territory – which also included Jaffah, Haifa and Ramleh – with only 300 knights. This required diplomacy and tolerance as well as force. When Edessa fell in 1144 and the Second Crusade was launched to retake it, the new crusaders were appalled that the Christian rulers had not converted all the Muslims or torn down the mosques, and that unbelievers were allowed into the churches. The crusade duly failed because of the divisions that opened within the Christian forces.

By the late twelfth century, Egypt and Syria were reunited under Saladin, a remarkable leader who was admired even by his Christian enemies.

TIMELINE	AD325–800	800–1100
When the Roman Empire fell, the peace it had imposed on Europe collapsed, and several chaotic centuries passed before any powers arose which could offer the continent a comparable degree of stability. The later Middle Ages saw power in Europe shared between the twin pillars of the Holy Roman Empire and the papacy, united by a common enmity towards Islam.	**364** Emperor Valentinian officially split the Roman Empire in two. **410** Visigoths, led by Alaric, sacked Rome. **c.496** Conversion of Clovis, King of the Franks. **506** Frankish conquest of Visigothic kingdom in southwest Gaul. **568** Lombard invasion of Italy. **570** Birth of Mohammed in Mecca. **597** Augustine of Canterbury began the conversion of Kent. **632** Death of Mohammed. **638** Fall of Jerusalem to Arabs. **711** Arab conquest of Iberian peninsula began. **732** Frankish leader Charles Martel defeated Arab forces at Poitiers, France. **772** First of Charlemagne's campaigns against the Saxons. **778** Charlemagne's forces defeated at Roncesvalles. **800** Charlemagne crowned as Holy Roman Emperor.	**814** Louis the Pious succeeded Charlemagne. **843** Carolingian empire dismembered into three kingdoms by the Treaty of Verdun. **c.886–1025** A Macedonian Renaissance occurred in Byzantium. **909** Monastery at Cluny founded by William the Pious of Aquitaine. **1016** Cnut of Denmark became king of England and, three years later, Denmark. **1035** Count Ramon Berenguer I of Barcelona expanded Catalan lands and influence in the Pyrenees in the wake of the Treaty of Verdun. **1054** Patriarch of Constantinople denounced the Roman Church, splitting the Orthodox and Catholic traditions. **1066** Duke William of Normandy defeated King Harold of England at Hastings, thereby commencing the Norman Conquest of England. **1071** Seljuk Turks defeated Byzantine forces. **1085** Castilian forces captured Toledo. **1095** Urban II proclaimed the First Crusade. **1099** Jerusalem fell to the crusaders. Spanish hero, El Cid, died.

Bronze Roman helmet found in Judah, 1st–3rd century AD.

In many ways he was a chivalric figure. At a time when massacres were commonplace, he opposed them and pointed out that "spilt blood never slumbers". He was a brilliant commander and his defeat of the Knights Templar at Tiberias in 1187 was the beginning of the end of Christian rule in Palestine. The crusaders set out to relieve the city but were surrounded at Hattin where, short of water and trapped on terrain unsuited to cavalry, they were decisively beaten. Within a few months Saladin had retaken Jerusalem, giving its defenders safe passage back to Christian territories.

A Third Crusade was preached. One army, led from Germany by Frederick I Barbarossa, took the overland route and was decimated as it passed through Asia Minor, but other forces – of the English king, Richard the Lionheart, and the French ruler, Philip II Augustus – arrived by sea and succeeded in taking Acre and Jaffah. The two monarchs quarrelled incessantly, however, and Philip abandoned the crusade in 1191, using the opportunity to attack Richard's lands in Aquitaine and Normandy. When Richard left the Holy Land the following year, he was captured by Leopold, Duke of Austria and held to ransom by Leopold's overlord, Emperor Henry VI. The unity and protection under the Church which all crusaders were supposed to enjoy had crumbled totally.

Further crusades were mostly disastrous, often not even reaching the Holy Land. Emperor Frederick II led an expedition in 1227, persuading the Sultan of Egypt to surrender Jerusalem, Bethlehem and Nazareth, but his successes were achieved largely by diplomacy – and at the time he was excommunicated for his efforts. The most embarrassing event of all for the Church was the Fourth Crusade, in which the crusaders sold their services to the Doge of Venice and a Byzantine pretender to the throne. Instead of marching to Jerusalem they sacked Constantinople. Men calling themselves "soldiers of Christ" stole holy relics and made the split between the Greek Orthodox and Roman churches irrevocable.

The West never stopped searching for new allies to guard against the Muslim threat, however. In 1241 the Mongols swept through southeastern Europe as far as the Dalmatian coast, before retreating again with equally surprising speed.

Norman mosaic from the Church of Martorana in Palermo, Sicily, of George of Antioch, admiral to King Roger II, c.12th century.

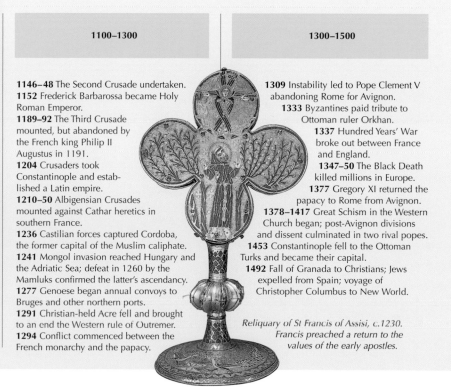

1100–1300	1300–1500

1146–48 The Second Crusade undertaken.
1152 Frederick Barbarossa became Holy Roman Emperor.
1189–92 The Third Crusade mounted, but abandoned by the French king Philip II Augustus in 1191.
1204 Crusaders took Constantinople and established a Latin empire.
1210–50 Albigensian Crusades mounted against Cathar heretics in southern France.
1236 Castilian forces captured Cordoba, the former capital of the Muslim caliphate.
1241 Mongol invasion reached Hungary and the Adriatic Sea; defeat in 1260 by the Mamluks confirmed the latter's ascendancy.
1277 Genoese began annual convoys to Bruges and other northern ports.
1291 Christian-held Acre fell and brought to an end the Western rule of Outremer.
1294 Conflict commenced between the French monarchy and the papacy.

1309 Instability led to Pope Clement V abandoning Rome for Avignon.
1333 Byzantines paid tribute to Ottoman ruler Orkhan.
1337 Hundred Years' War broke out between France and England.
1347–50 The Black Death killed millions in Europe.
1377 Gregory XI returned the papacy to Rome from Avignon.
1378–1417 Great Schism in the Western Church began; post-Avignon divisions and dissent culminated in two rival popes.
1453 Constantinople fell to the Ottoman Turks and became their capital.
1492 Fall of Granada to Christians; Jews expelled from Spain; voyage of Christopher Columbus to New World.

Reliquary of St Francis of Assisi, c.1230. Francis preached a return to the values of the early apostles.

A number of opportunistic bishops began to wonder if they could be used to destroy the Islamic world, but in an ironic historical twist it was the Muslim Mamluks of Egypt who saved the West from the Mongols. Under Hulagu, the brother of Kublai Khan, the Mongols sacked Baghdad and Damascus before again sweeping westwards towards the Mediterranean, only to be crushed by the Mamluks in 1260 at Ain Jalut, near Gaza.

A Feudal Society

At home, medieval European society was rigidly hierarchical. Below the king and the feudal nobility were the churchmen, the warriors, and then peasants and labourers. Reaching its height in the eleventh and twelfth centuries, the system of feudalism was the foundation of the entire medieval world, accounting for both its social structure and its means of waging continual warfare, not least in a series of dynastic conflicts in the fourteenth century, notably the Hundred Years' War, which served to reinforce the national monarchical identities of both France and England. Importantly, feudalism was also central to the evolution of cultured notions of knighthood and the chivalric code, the existence of which, in turn, assisted and then reinforced the code of courtly love and the entire genre of romance literature. The seeds of feudalism, however, had germinated for some centuries before flowering.

Before the second half of the eighth century, a king might make a grant of land to one of his subjects, in full ownership and for the lifetime of the tenant. From the time of the Frankish rulers, however, this type of benefice was replaced by the granting of fiefs. In this case, the king retained ownership of the land, but allowed his tenant extensive rights over it in return for the promise of certain payments or services. The tenant thereby became the vassal of the king.

In the early days of the system, the vassal's main duty was service as a knight. He had to pledge himself, his warhorses, his

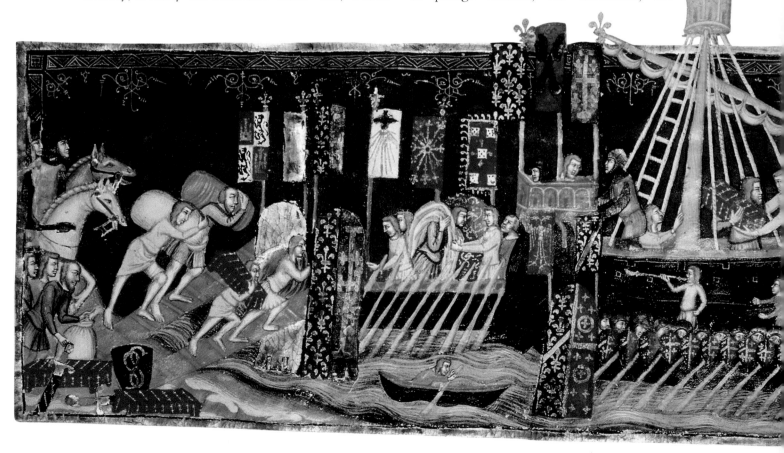

weapons and armour – and often those of his followers – for a fixed amount of time (typically forty days) each year. If the king was not fighting a war, the service might involve guarding a castle or riding escort. By the twelfth century, the knight's service was increasingly replaced by a more straight-forward monetary payment known as scutage, and although originally only kings granted fiefs in return for vassalage, the practice was eventually taken up by lesser nobility too.

The feudal system was carried by the Franks into Italy, Spain and Germany, and by the Normans into England and Sicily. Oppressed by the military service expected of them by the Crown, free peasants would often surrender their few acres to their lord if he relieved them of the responsibility, and so the manors grew ever larger. As the feudal lords became stronger, monarchs themselves were threatened. This was the age of great warrior barons whose power struggles with rulers were continual. It also spurred the popularity of literature which drew upon heroic ideals, from the ancients such as Alexander onwards.

The amalgamation of estates was also a product of marriage or warfare. A typical manor contained a fortified manor house, the village which housed the peasants, three fields worked in rotation (with one left fallow each year) and uncultivated land which provided hay, forage and wood.

Ships are loaded in preparation for their departure on the First Crusade in 1096, from the French manuscript *Status de l'Ordre du St Esprit*.

Some land was leased to free tenants, either for a rent or in return for military service, while the rest was worked by serfs or villeins. Although the serf was not free, could own no property and was not allowed to leave the manor, he was not a slave because he could not be bought or sold and had certain rights determined by local conventions. Usually he worked several strips of land, living off the produce and in return paying a fee of money, crops or livestock. In addition, he had to work the lord's property for him.

With all the work being done by the lower classes, the landed gentry found time to promote the arts. They developed a culture and literature that served to reinforce their own narrow view of the world, elaborating a stylized code of behaviour in which honour and duty were elevated to a quasi-religious status and women were ascribed a very defined role as objects of men's desires. There were two principal centres of artistic output: at the Parisian court Frankish, chivalric *chansons de geste* were popularized, centred initially on the cult of Charlemagne (especially *Chanson de Roland*); the court of Aquitaine at Poitiers, meanwhile, specialized in promoting songs of courtly love or *chansons d'amour*, derived from earlier troubadour poetry, and, particularly after 1120, elaborating the code of courtly romance whose master was Chretien de Troyes. The rules of this social and poetic game gave the lead to the mistress of the knight's affections and thereby subversively reversed the generally accepted gender roles of the day, flouting matrimonial convention. (Ironically, however, one widespread attraction of a considerable amount of courtly literature was that it was composed in reaction against the boorish lifestyle of the large, land-owning barons and the stifling ethics of the Church.)

The Rise of the Monasteries

Until eclipsed by the increasingly secular universities which in the thirteenth century rose to challenge their monopoly on the dissemination of knowledge, the monasteries were among Europe's most powerful institutions and a dominant cultural force in the shaping of the continent. Monks were also instrumental in writing down many of the traditional romances that had earlier existed in purely oral form; in so doing, they often gave them a Christian gloss.

Almost without exception, the feudal lords of the eleventh and twelfth centuries shared a passion for establishing monasteries. Thousands were built across Europe, sometimes in the superstitious hope of relieving a plague or a crop failure. More often, though, the patron was simply attracted by the idea of having a community nearby engaged in constant prayer, interceding with God on behalf of the living and the dead. It helped too – both from the nobles' and the monks' points of view – that the intensively hard work monks undertook in the fields served to reclaim lands that would otherwise have remained unproductive.

Monasticism, in the sense of religious communities separated from secular distractions, had an ancient pedigree in Christianity with prestigious communities taking root as far apart as Italy and Scotland, but the rules of the movement were only really established by Benedict of Nursia in the sixth century. He wanted to create a "school for beginners" on the road to a selfless life, where ordinary people could learn to live apart from the world while enduring "nothing harsh nor burdensome". A monastery had to be a self-sufficient and independent community. When someone became a monk he renounced all property and submitted to the will of God and the rest of the brotherhood. The most important virtues were obedience and humility, which were taught by a strict regime of prayer and agricultural labour.

By the tenth century, however, some monastic orders considered the Benedictine rules to be only the minimum condition for a monkish life. They believed in a much longer and more arduous programme of meditation, prayer and psalm-singing, which left them with no time for such earthly pursuits as working in the fields. They were able to undertake this ascetic life because of their rich patrons, who endowed them not only with cultivated land but also with attendant serfs. The monasteries came to resemble feudal manors in their own right. As their wealth grew and manual labour diminished, they played an increasingly important part in preserving the culture of the Christian West, especially through the painstaking work of copying and illuminating old manuscripts.

Peasants working on a feudal estate in a scene illustrating the month of March from the Limbourg brothers' *Tres Riches Heures du Duc de Berry*, early 15th century.

The Black Death

Epidemics have ravaged Europe since the first conquering armies, and the first merchants, brought back diseases from distant lands for which their countrymen had no natural immunity. But the most devastating plague of all came from Asia during the fourteenth century.

The Black Death that spread throughout Europe between 1347 and 1350 was bubonic plague, probably brought back from the Far East aboard Italian merchants' ships. It was transmitted by fleas that lived in the fur of black rats, and could be recognized by the attendant purple blotches and lumps, called buboes. It attacked the lymph glands and the nervous system, and was fatal in more than half of all cases. There was also a pneumonic strain that attacked the lungs and was even more deadly.

It is estimated that more than thirty per cent of Europe's population was wiped out in three years by the Black Death.

Entire villages were destroyed or deserted, and in many large towns there were not enough healthy people to bury the dead. Frequent outbreaks of plague recurred for more than a century, and the massive social upheaval that accompanied them led to widespread penitential cults and a subversive attitude which questioned authority and the teachings of the Church. With labour demand intensified, it also contributed to a host of popular uprisings, including the English Peasants' Revolt of 1381.

Burial of plague victims in Tournai, France, in 1349, from a 14th-century Flemish book illustration.

One of the most important orders, the Cistercians, was established in the last years of the eleventh century as a response to this otherworldliness. The Cistercians wanted to return to the pure, austere observance proposed by Benedict, worshipping according to his rules and reviving the practice of arduous agricultural work. Consequently, they built their monasteries far from the material comforts of human habitation, in uncultivated moorland or remote forest. Despite their attempts to live almost as hermits, however, the Cistercians became famous, partly because one of their members, Bernard, was a visionary and a rhetorical genius who wrote scathing attacks on the wealth of the other orders. When he joined the religious order in 1112 it had only one abbey, in Citeaux, France, but when he died in 1153 there were more than 300. Many abbeys guarded holy relics, while others sheltered and fed pilgrims en route to visit shrines (see pages 28–31). Although they prayed less than other orders, the Cistercians gained a reputation for holiness because of their poverty and asceticism. Ironically, in the process they began to attract more gifts and bequests which in time made them rich, undermining their original ideals.

The Rise of Commerce

By the twelfth and thirteenth centuries – when medieval culture flourished, with Gothic architecture, education and legal systems ascendant – the whole feudal system was in a state of decline. At this time the wealth of a country increasingly lay not in its land but in its trade. Towns were expanding and becoming more powerful, passing their own laws and often hiring their own armies, thus eroding the very basis of feudalism. The idea of a bonded lord-vassal relationship was being replaced by the concept of a sovereign and his subjects or, more revolutionarily, a citizen and the body elected to represent him. Social units, from guilds to civic councils, flourished.

In addition, the volume of trade meant that Europe's economy was inflationary, while the feudal lords were living on estates that, for centuries, had provided them with a fixed income. If they clung to past ways, they faced the prospect of becoming poorer and poorer in relation to many of their own increasingly prosperous subjects. Indeed, the fuel for many other developments, from church-building to the crusades, was economic growth and wealth, both rural and urban.

The growth of towns was fuelled by a massive population explosion from the eleventh century onwards as lands were reclaimed and forests cut down all over western Europe. In the past, most towns had been little more than fortified

Workers carting wheat to market in a scene from the *Luttrell Psalter*, 14th century. The rise in trade marked the beginning of the end of medieval feudal society, for the future would lie in the hands of merchants, not warriors.

settlements, built to defend some strategic point such as a river crossing, but now they were based around a marketplace, or occasionally around an important shrine or site of pilgrimage. At first local lords sought to profit by taxing the markets, but as the towns grew in size and power, the citizens began to resent this. They asked for "commune" status, which gave them the right, through civic councils, to govern themselves. Early in the twelfth century, the townspeople of Laon murdered their bishop when he refused. Increasingly nervous lords began selling charters to the towns on their territory, which at least gave them some compensation for their loss of power.

In this way, the communes acquired a power comparable to that of the feudal barons, with their own territory and courts. Although they claimed their authority came from "the people gathered in assembly", they were not truly democratic institutions for they were ruled exclusively by important families. Nevertheless, any serf who managed to stay in a town for a year and a day legally gained his freedom, although this did not mean that he could work as he wished. The manufacture, buying and selling of goods were strictly controlled by guilds, which rose to prominence from the eleventh century onwards. They were enormously wealthy and powerful institutions, which in many cases had their own police forces and jails, paid for by a weekly subscription that each guild levied from all its members. The funds were also used to provide money for colleagues who became sick, to pay for Masses for the dead, to provide pensions for widows and to stage elaborate pageants on holy days.

The guild not only regulated its members and protected them from competition; it also controlled wages and prices and set the standards by which an apprentice progressed to become a master of his craft. There were usually prohibitions against inventing new tools or techniques, or using the unpaid labour of wives and children. Merchants as well as craftsmen had their own guilds, and no manufactured goods could be imported from other towns except during a fair.

A guild acted as a monopoly whose members would all lower their wages at the same time, or raise prices simultaneously when raw materials became scarce. They would also act together to freeze out troublesome workers, who were much more militant and organized in towns than their feudal counterparts. In the countryside, with the exception of occasional albeit serious uprisings, there was very little opposition to the lord of the manor, for a refusal to work meant starvation. In the towns, however, workers regularly downed tools if their wages were in arrears, or organized themselves into gangs to intimidate any who might be prepared to work for less than the standard rate.

Towns did not necessarily rely on trade for all their wealth. Some were pilgrimage sites, or the homes of saints, and could make a fortune from tourism or by selling relics. Some built universities and attracted wealthy students to swell their economy. Others exploited the growing poverty of the feudal nobility by mortgaging their lands, and money was also lent in huge amounts to the Church in order to fund its ambitious building programme. The vast majority of the surviving cathedrals and major churches in western Europe were built during the high medieval period.

The new secular, bourgeois class also gave its blessing to fresh influences, and in the arts there was the growth of an irreverent genre of carvings, ballads and writings which delighted in making fun of the new rich and the pompously powerful governing classes.

Scene from the *Roman de Gerhard de Roussillon* showing masons building churches, 14th century. Gothic architecture remains one of the most visible legacies of the medieval age.

The medieval towns witnessed the birth of much that we would recognize in society today – from representative government and labour unions to merchant banks and further education. The period influenced many aspects of culture that we take for granted, including languages, architecture, organized nation states and folk heroes. It also left a huge canon of literature which still informs and affects modern artistic genres, from crafts to theatre and cinema.

PATHS OF THE PILGRIMS

In the year AD326, Helena, mother of the Roman emperor Constantine, visited the Holy Land believing the long and arduous trip would cleanse the sin of her family. In doing so she laid the foundations of one of the most significant rituals of the medieval Christian Church: pilgrimage – and also, by promoting the building of basilicas and establishing shrines, mapped out the sites mentioned in the Bible. The trip to Jerusalem thereafter became an act of worship in itself, the spiritual high point of a Christian's life. After the Holy Land fell to the Saracens in 1244, other destinations gained in importance – and one such, Santiago de Compostela in Spain, has never lost its pulling power. For the heritage of the medieval pilgrim survives to this day, when pilgrimage remains a major part of the lives of millions of Christians.

Left: St Helena is credited with establishing the tradition of pilgrimage by elevating the importance of the holy sites mentioned in the New Testament. Despite some dissenting voices in the Church, the tradition flourished. Painting by Giovanni dal Ponte, *c*.1420.

Left: Pilgrims en route to Canterbury, stained glass from Canterbury Cathedral, 13th century. On the road, social station was supposedly put aside, subsumed by the spiritual equality of Christian fellowship. But not all people went by horse or on foot. Wealthier pilgrims would travel by carriage and would regard their vehicle as a moveable chapel.

Below: Canterbury was one of the holiest venues in England. It became a key site in the eyes of the Church after the murder of Thomas Becket in 1170, an event which led to the archbishop's canonization. Although Henry VIII later destroyed Becket's shrine, which he saw as a symbol of resistance to royal authority, many elaborately decorated caskets survived to commemorate his martyrdom, such as this one from Limoges in France, *c.*1180.

Above left: Just as holy sites grew in importance, so too relics gained in spiritual significance. Revered objects could include pieces of the Cross or parts of a saint's body. Relics were seen as physical manifestations of saints, so reliquaries, such as this 13th-century silver gilt hand from Flanders, became portable shrines. A saint's bones would have been visible in the glass "rings" on the object's fingers.

Left: The Holy Land's importance was symbolic rather than strategic, and the crusades were seen at the time by those who undertook them as a sort of armed pilgrimage. Here Godfrey de Bouillon captures Jerusalem in 1099, from the *Chronique d'Outre Mer*, 14th century.

Above: The consecration of the monastery at Cluny, in France, by Pope Urban II, from a 14th-century manuscript. Monasteries became important sponsors of pilgrimages, establishing a network of routes throughout Europe. Cluny was one of the most prominent, organizing journeys to Santiago de Compostela. Such patronage was important since the long routes were hazardous and pilgrims had to be prepared practically as well as spiritually for the trek.

Right: The Cathedral in Santiago de Compostela, the spectacular destination of most pilgrims to Spain. The city became the third most holy place in Christendom after Jerusalem and Rome. The cathedral dates from the 12–13th centuries but the baroque *Obradoiro* facade is 18th century. From the ceiling inside the famous *botafumeiro,* a giant incense burner, is swung above the altar, while at the door stands the *Santos dos Croques,* the statue which pilgrims still touch for good luck just as they did eight centuries ago.

Left: Statue of St James in his familiar guise as a pilgrim, with staff and scallop shell. Legend has it that James, the cousin of Christ, made his way to Santiago after the crucifixion and that his body was buried on the site of the later cathedral. St James is sometimes represented as the less gentle *Matamoros,* the "killer of the Moors", riding a horse and carrying a mighty sword in his hand.

Far left: The rugged hills around Covadonga in Asturias presented many days' hard walking to pilgrims who had possibly already come hundreds of kilometres. The area still boasts an abundance of local shrines to offer spiritual succour to the weary. A cave in the mountains shelters an image of Our Lady of Covadonga, celebrating an 8th-century Christian victory over the Moors. This remains a point of pilgrimage in itself and each year crowds gather to pay homage to the patron saint of Asturias.

THE HEROES OF EPIC

In AD778 Charlemagne led an army from France over the Pyrenees mountain range into Spain, where he laid siege to the Muslim-held city of Saragossa (modern Zaragoza). Despite his seemingly invincible force, however, Charlemagne failed to take the city, and after an unsatisfactory campaign he resolved to retreat to France. On the way, in a narrow mountain pass near Roncesvalles, the rear of his army was attacked and defeated. His nephew, Roland, died in what may have been no more than a minor skirmish – but his name was made immortal in heroic song.

Dating from the late eleventh century, the *Chanson de Roland* ("Song of Roland") that commemorates Roland's death is the earliest surviving example of the medieval French *chansons de geste* ("songs of great deeds"). These were a series of epics that recounted the glorious exploits of Christian knights in the service of Charlemagne and his descendants. They portray warriors defending Christendom against the soldiers of Islam – who were often called "Saracens", from the Arabic *sharqiyin* ("Easterners").

The *chanson de geste* manuscripts date mostly from the twelfth to the fifteenth centuries, but many scholars believe the poems developed in an oral tradition and may have been popular for around 200 years before they were written down. Their influence throughout Europe was immense, for they fed both into the heroic poetry of Spain, which bore rich fruit in the twelfth-century poem about the Spanish nobleman El Cid called *Cantar de Mio Cid* ("Song of My Cid"), and into fifteenth- and sixteenth-century Italian verse about Charlemagne and his knights by writers such as Boiardo and Ariosto (see page 44).

The *chansons* are the earliest manifestation of the literature of chivalry, a great body of medieval work that encompassed epic cycles, ballads and prose romances celebrating honour, loyalty and the heroic encounters in war and love of knights and their ladies.

And these tales were not restricted to Christian heroes, for many of the great figures of the classical world were adopted as paragons of chivalric honour. Such was the destiny of the fourth-century BC Macedonian Alexander the Great, whose cult, embroidered with legend, enjoyed a popular revival in medieval times.

Opposite: In the Middle Ages, Charlemagne was held up as the exemplar of chivalric honour, mixing military skill and Christian morality. Here he leads his men against the Muslims in Spain. Painting by Antoine Verard, *c.*15th century.

Below: Stained glass image of the royal arms of England, early 14th-century. Heraldry was one of the most distinctive features of the age of chivalry.

Charlemagne and the Song of Roland

Charlemagne and his noble knights had spent long, successful years fighting the Saracens in Spain. But as they travelled home, assured of an enduring peace, disaster struck – and, most tragically of all, the seeds of the calamity were sown in the Christian camp.

The *Chanson de Roland* is derived from the historical facts of Charlemagne's invasion of Spain in 778, but only distantly – for its stirring account of chivalrous warriors defending the Christian world against Muslim hordes is legend. Charlemagne was thirty-six at the time of the invasion, but in the poem he becomes a venerable 200-year-old and his brief Spanish campaign is made to last seven years. Furthermore, at the poem's start, of all the cities in Spain, only Saragossa continues to defy the Christian army whereas, in fact, most of the country remained under Muslim control.

The story begins with Marsiliun, ruler of Saragossa, debating with his nobles how best to resist the Franks. One of them, Blancandrin, proposed a trick: Marsiliun should send Charlemagne word that he vowed to visit him at his French palace in Aix later in the year and, at the festival of Michaelmas, convert to Christianity; he should back the promise up with hostages and sweeten it with gifts of camels and bears, lions and falcons and gold from Arabia itself. If the plan worked, Charlemagne would return to France and leave Spain alone. When Marsiliun then failed to appear in Aix, Charlemagne would slaughter the hostages – but that would be a small price to pay for the continued freedom of their sweet land of Spain.

This plan pleased Marsiliun and he swiftly dispatched Blancandrin and nine other messengers to set this lie to work. They found Charlemagne encamped at Cordes, in France. The king held court in an orchard on a golden throne, his long white beard flowing over his broad chest. Around him stood the twelve great warriors or paladins of his court, who included Charlemagne's nephew, brave Roland, and Roland's close companion, Oliver, whose sister Alde Roland favoured with his love; then there were Anseis and Gefrey of Anjou, standard-bearer to the king. All about Charlemagne were his 15,000 followers, testing their prowess at swordplay or their wits over chess, and all joyous to serve so noble a lord.

Islamic rulers maintained a presence in Spain from AD756 until almost the 16th century. Here, the emir of Cordoba, one of Charlemagne's enemies, consults his courtiers, from a 14th-century manuscript.

Into this company, then, came deceitful Blancandrin and his fellow delegates. He repeated the duplicitous message he had prepared, promising Charlemagne magnificent gifts and noble hostages as proof of Marsiliun's good intent.

The following morning, after hearing services in praise of God, Charlemagne called his nobles to him to seek their counsel. Roland spoke out at once, urging the king to reject the offer. Ganelon pressed the king to accept, arguing that the chance of an honourable peace was a sweeter prospect for them all than the risk of death in continuing the war. The Duke of Naimes agreed with Ganelon, and the king then asked who should carry this decision to the Muslim leader.

Roland offered to take the message, but Oliver voiced his fear that his friend's pride would lead him into conflict in the enemy's camp. So Roland suggested that his stepfather Ganelon should carry the king's word to Marsiliun and the knights hailed this as a wise choice.

A pass in the Pyrenees in Aragon, near Zaragoza (Saragossa). Charlemagne's army had already crossed the mountains by the time Roland and his band of warriors were ambushed.

Cowardly Ganelon quaked inwardly with fear. He felt duty-bound to accept the commission, but he quietly cursed Roland, promising he would take revenge by trickery.

Mounting his charger, Ganelon rode away with Blancandrin and his party. As they went he once more gave vent to his bitterness against Roland, while crafty Blancandrin egged him on. In the low voice of conspirators they swiftly came to an understanding – they would work together to bring about Roland's downfall.

When Ganelon first came into Marsiliun's presence, he spoke proudly and provoked a confrontation for appearances' sake. But at a private meeting between the Muslim king and the Christian messenger Marsiliun offered sumptuous bribes, which Ganelon was happy to accept.

Two knights in combat, from a 15th-century chronicle. As was traditional in chivalric warfare, battle commenced with individuals engaging in single combat. The Battle of Roncesvalles began with Roland challenging Aelroth, Marsiliun's nephew.

Ganelon then proposed an attack on the rear of Charlemagne's army as it retreated through the mountains to France. He would arrange it so that Roland and Oliver would be commanding this small force, which could be defeated with ease. Roland would be dispatched and Charlemagne would grieve the loss as bitterly as that of his own right arm. Then, having made a vow to betray Roland to the Muslim king, Ganelon returned to his master, leading a train of 700 camels bearing gold and silver along with the twenty hostages.

The Frankish king was deceived by Ganelon's treachery and ordered his army to set out on the road to France. As it marched, a great host of Saracen warriors settled on the wooded slopes of the mountains, preparing to attack.

Night fell and Charlemagne was troubled by portentous dreams, but he knew that the army had set its path and there was no going back. In the light of morning he consulted with his lords as to who should command the rearguard of the army through the mountains and Ganelon spoke up eagerly, naming Roland for the duty. Charlemagne, knowing that the rearguard would be vulnerable to attack, responded bitterly, accusing Ganelon of devilish intent. But fearless Roland was honour-bound to accept the nomination.

Charlemagne and the main part of the army travelled on through the Pyrenees. When they reached France they waited, but fears for Roland's safety tormented the king. Meanwhile, in the mountain pass, Roland prepared for battle.

A Deadly Ambush

High in the peaks, Marsiliun's knights girded their limbs in shining armour. They sounded their trumpets, and the deathly noise carried to the Franks in the pass of Roncesvalles.

When Oliver saw the vast Saracen army massed on the steep hillsides around them, he urged Roland to sound his ivory horn to recall the main Frankish army to their aid. But Roland declared that seeking help would bring shame upon them all. Four times Oliver asked Roland to sound the alarm; four times he declined.

Roland then spoke to his men, urging them to fight hard for the glory of God and their king and to ensure that their own knightly reputation suffered no blemish. Archbishop Turpin rode forward and proclaimed the approaching battle to be a holy one; the souls of those who fell in defence of the Christian faith, he promised, would be transported swiftly from the battlefield to Paradise.

Then the Christian knights raised King Charlemagne's battle-cry of "Mountjoy!" and advanced with bursting hearts. Twelve Saracen champions came forward to meet their Christian counterparts. The first combat was between Marsiliun's nephew, Aelroth, and great Roland himself: Roland's lance skewered the Saracen knight, breaking open his chest and snapping his neck, and he flung him like a carcass onto the ground. Next, with similar force, Oliver unseated and killed Duke Fulsarun, one of Marsiliun's brothers. God appeared to be bringing victory to his Christian champions: Archbishop Turpin, Gerin, Gerer, Duke Sansun, Anseis, Engeler and Otun all rode to victory. Of the twelve Saracen knights, only one, Margarit of Seville, won.

The Franks had fought their enemies to a standstill, but then a second wave of Marsiliun's army rode forward along the mountain valleys and with shuddering impact came up against the Christians. One by one, the leading Frankish knights were felled.

Roland, seeing his army brought low, proposed to blow his ivory horn to summon Charlemagne to their aid. But now Oliver called this an act of cowardice. He indicated the hosts of fallen Frankish knights around them, and that their death was Roland's doing – for if he had used the horn before to bring Charlemagne back they would have triumphed in battle and their lives would have been spared. Never again, he declared, would he allow Roland to pay court to his fair sister Alde. Roland's overconfidence had led him astray: now, because of Roland's pride in his reputation, they would die, the army would be devastated and the reputation of France itself would be stained.

Hearing words of anger, Archbishop Turpin rode up to the knights and counselled them to lay aside their differences. He advised blowing the horn; it would be too late to save them, but it would bring the Frankish forces back to the battlefield where they could tend to the corpses of the fallen, which would otherwise be left out beneath the sun like those of mere animals.

Then Roland set the horn singing in the thin mountain air; far away in the French foothills of the mighty Pyrenees Charlemagne and his army heard it. The emperor leaped to his feet, declaring

that his nephew must be hard-pressed in battle. Ganelon tried to dismiss the claim: no one, he declared, would dare fight Roland – the fearless lord must be blowing the horn in sport.

At Roncesvalles, Roland blew until the veins burst on his forehead. In France, Charlemagne ordered his troops to arm, mount and ride back to try to save Roland's life. He now realized Ganelon's treachery and in fury ordered him to be seized, bound and turned into the care of the travelling cooks of the royal household. They were happy to give the traitor a good beating and when they were finished they flung him over a mule like mere baggage.

The Franks rode hard to the battlefield, but they were too late to save any of their compatriots at Roncesvalles – for just sixty Frankish knights were left alive. Yet still they fought heroically against overwhelming odds.

Marganice, Marsiliun's uncle and the lord of Ethiopia and Carthage, came late on to the battlefield with a great host of African soldiers. He drove his spear into Oliver's body, but the Frankish knight fought back with his great sword Halteclere, cleaving Marganice's head in two. Death had come close to Oliver, but in a frenzy of pain he charged back into the thick of battle.

There he encountered Roland, but because his eyesight was now failing he did not recognize his friend. Mistaking him for an enemy, he hacked

With armies stretched out across either side of the Pyrenees, the only means of communication was by the horn. But when Roland finally tried to summon Charlemagne's troops to his aid, he found he had left it too late. Ivory and silver horn, c.12th century.

at his helmet with Halteclere. The great sword sliced through the metal but did not harm Roland. Then the Frankish hero, astonished, identified himself – and Oliver, at last recognizing his friend's voice, begged forgiveness, explaining that he could no longer see. Roland understood that Oliver was close to death and he called God as his witness that he forgave his companion for the assault. (Bruising conflicts between comrades in arms who had failed to recognize each other were a common occurrence in the *chansons de geste*.)

Oliver felt the end of his earthly life upon him. He dismounted and, reclining on the blood-soaked field, earnestly confessed his sins. His soul departed, and Roland knew the deepest grief that man ever felt. For a moment he fainted in the saddle, yet quickly recovered and fought on.

So fierce to behold were Roland, Archbishop Turpin and a third Frank named Gualter of Hum that the Saracen hordes held back, throwing spears and javelins from a distance. Gualter was killed by one of these, and Archbishop Turpin was struck and his horse dispatched.

Roland, who was growing weak, blew a feeble note on the horn; the returning Franks, hearing it, understood that the battle was almost lost. Archbishop Turpin then took a mighty blow to the head and four spears struck his body.

In the last attack of the battle 400 Saracens rode against Roland. They killed his horse and destroyed his helmet but they could not break his spirit. Then the Saracens heard the main Frankish contingent returning and they all fled in fear. Roland and Archbishop Turpin seemed to be the only living men on the battlefield.

The archbishop was too weak to stand, but Roland, distraught with grief, walked across the gore-drenched slopes of Roncesvalles seeking the bodies of his closest comrades. One by one he found them and laid them out beside the archbishop. When Roland fainted once more, Turpin summoned the last vestiges of his strength to rise and fetch the knight some much-needed water. But the archbishop collapsed and, lying on his back, gazed up into the clear air above him and commended his soul to God in Heaven.

The Battle of Roncesvalles in History and Myth

Scholars know almost nothing for certain about the historical battle that forms the centrepiece of the Chanson de Roland.

The historical evidence for the confrontation at Roncesvalles is contradictory. One contemporary chronicle, the *Annales Royales,* refers to the 778 campaign in Spain but makes no mention of a battle in the Pyrenees. When the annals were revised about twenty-five years later, however, they included an account of a trek through the Pyrenees during which Basques hid in the mountains and attacked the rear of Charlemagne's army, killing its commanders and looting the baggage train.

One of Charlemagne's biographers, the monk Einhard (*c.*770–840), portrayed the mountain battle as a minor defeat which he blamed on the treachery of the Gascons. Among those killed in it he named Hroudland (Roland), Warden of the Breton Marches, Egginhard, the royal seneschal, and Anselm, Count of the Palace. A biography of Charlemagne's son, Louis, written about sixty years after 778, mentioned the battle and remarked that the names of those who perished were so well known as to need no repetition. By that stage, the combat had evidently gained an important position in popular legend, however insignificant it had been in reality.

Modern scholars often suggest that the truth may lie in a combination of the various accounts of the battle. Most argue that a clash which assumed such importance in popular memory was surely more than the minor and unimportant skirmish suggested by early chronicle accounts. They point to the fact that the day after the battle Charlemagne reorganized the defences of Aquitaine, suggesting that the defeat had

Then Roland came once more to his senses and, taking up his horn and his sword, Durendal, he staggered to his feet. He came to a promontory where he fainted again. A Saracen who had been feigning death saw his chance. He ran forward and tried to wrench the weapon from the Christian knight's grasp, but Roland recovered his strength and lashed out with his horn. His blow was so heavy that it split his assailant's skull.

Roland knew that the hour of his death was close. With his last energy, he prayed that God might keep Durendal from the hands of cowards. Then, beneath a tall pine, he laid out his sword and his horn and stretched himself on top of them. He set his face towards Spain and his enemies as a sign that he died unconquered. With his final breath he begged God's forgiveness and raised his right glove to Heaven. Then angels came to conduct him to his celestial home.

When the Frankish contingent finally reached Roncesvalles they wept at the sight. Leaving a small detachment to watch over the fallen, Charlemagne and his troops caught and defeated the retreating Saracens. Returning to the pass the next day they were surprised by another great Muslim army, newly arrived. But the Christian forces triumphed once more.

The Franks then marched home. At Blaye, just north of Bordeaux, the bodies of Roland, Oliver and Archbishop Turpin were buried with great ceremony beneath splendid white sarcophagi. Returning to his capital, Charlemagne was met by fair Alde, Oliver's sister who had hoped to become the wife of fearless Roland. Overcome with grief, the king passed on the tragic news that both these brave warriors were dead. The shock was too much for Alde and she fell down dead at the king's feet.

Later that year, before a great assembly in Aix, Ganelon was hanged and quartered – the dust of France was thirsty for his coward's blood. The same night Charlemagne was visited in his bedchamber by the Archangel Gabriel, calling him to another war in defence of Christendom.

been a major setback and he feared further attacks mounted from Spain – the reason why any weakening of the frontier March lands was so feared.

It may be that Christian Basques seeking revenge for the razing of Pamplona fought alongside Muslim soldiers. Some accounts suggest that Charlemagne took Suleiman ben al-Arabi, Emir of Barcelona, prisoner despite having supposedly gone to Spain to help the Muslim ruler, and this might have provoked an attack on Charlemagne's retreating army.

Charlemagne recovers the body of his nephew, Roland, after the Battle of Roncesvalles, from a 15th-century manuscript. The picture draws on legend rather than fact.

Huon and the Fairy King

The adventures of Duke Huon of Bordeaux form the basis of a late 12th-century *chanson de geste* which has a strong element of the fantastic. It is one of many songs describing the consequences of a quarrel between Charlemagne and his knights.

Duke Huon of Bordeaux had fallen out with the King of the Franks through a case of mistaken identity. Summoned to court, Huon had been ambushed at night by a group which included Charlemagne's wayward son, Charlot – and in the darkness Huon had killed him.

To atone for his misdeed, Huon was set a demanding task by Charlemagne: to travel to the court of Sultan Gaudys, Admiral of Babylon. There he had to decapitate the potentate's most illustrious guest, kiss his daughter three times and pluck his beard and four of his teeth as trophies.

Huon set sail with a company of knights. In Jerusalem, he visited Christ's tomb and prayed for God's protection. Then, in the desert beyond, he encountered a long-haired hermit. He was a French Christian, Gerames, who had been banished from France after killing a nobleman and had settled as a penitent. Gerames became one of Huon's party and pledged to show him the way to Babylon.

Gerames warned Huon that the shortest route lay through an enchanted forest that was ruled by Oberon, King of the Fairies. He urged avoiding it: Oberon's voice was sweet and his manner pleasant, but any who answered him was doomed to rest forever in that forest. Gerames' description only pricked Huon's curiosity and he resolved to travel that way.

The company encountered Oberon as soon as they reached the woods. He was no more than three feet tall and had the fresh twinkling eyes of a child; he wore a rich gown adorned with jewels. When he tried to make Huon and his knights speak to him, they all kept their silence. But, finally, Huon was moved to answer the fairy lord.

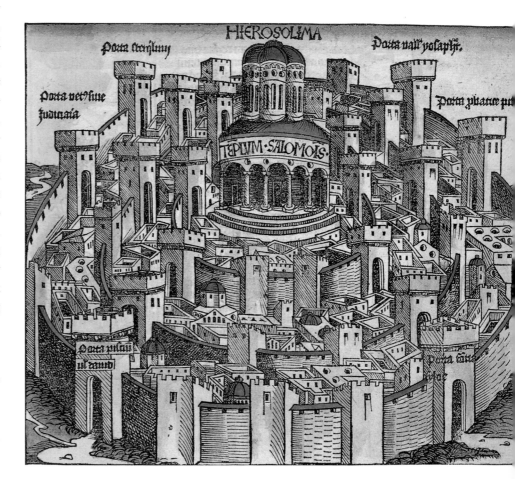

View of Jerusalem showing the Temple of Solomon and the city gates, from the *Nuremburg Chronicle*, c.1493. The city was seen as the physical and spiritual centre of the world and thus the object of personal quests, as well as the military goal of the crusades.

Oberon explained that Gerames had been mistaken in his fears. He presented Huon with a magic chalice that filled with wine when its bearer made the sign of the Cross over it. Only a Christian could drink from the chalice, he said, for the wine disappeared when the cup was held by a sinner.

In addition, he gave Huon an ivory horn telling him to blow it if he ever needed help: when its notes sounded, Oberon would appear with a great host of knights to support him. In parting, Oberon counselled Huon never to tell a lie – for if he did so he would forfeit Oberon's help.

Huon and his men rode on to many adventures. Huon slew a giant named Angolafer before coming alone to Babylon – in the poem an entirely legendary city on the River Nile, whose sacred waters flowed from Paradise itself. He penetrated the city's defences by showing the guards the ring he had cut from the finger of the feared giant, but at the first gate he lied when asked whether he were a Saracen. In that moment he forfeited Oberon's goodwill: later, when he blew on his magic horn, Oberon refused to come to his aid.

Huon gained admission to the admiral's palace and fulfilled the first two parts of his mission, striking off the head of the most prominent guest at the tables and kissing Admiral Gaudys' daughter, Claramond. But then he was overpowered and cast into a deep dungeon.

It was his good fortune that the touch of his lips had stirred the passion of the beautiful Claramond. She visited him in the prison and offered to help him; in return he agreed to marry her if she converted to the Christian faith, which she declared herself willing to do. She told her father that Huon had died in gaol, but all the time was plotting her escape to France with him.

Huon's knights and Gerames had remained at Angolafer's castle, but after a time they set out for Babylon to look for Huon. It happened that Angolafer's towering brother, Agrapart, also arrived in the city seeking revenge. He humiliated the admiral, knocking him from his throne and declaring him to be his subject unless he could produce a champion to contest his supremacy.

Byzantine goblet, pillaged from what is now Turkey. The chalice given to Huon by Oberon may have been infused with pagan magic, but it fulfilled a Christian purpose: an abundant source of wine, it would dry up if the drinker was a sinner.

None of Gaudys's knights dared fight the giant, so Claramond admitted her deception and produced Huon from prison as a possible champion. The admiral was happy to accept him, and the contest was arranged. The Christian knight won and Admiral Gaudys laid on a great feast.

Huon did not forget his commission from Charlemagne. He produced the chalice that Oberon had given him and showed Gaudys its magic, but when he handed it to the pagan lord the wine disappeared. Huon declared that it had happened because Gaudys was not a Christian and tried to convert him to the faith, but Gaudys was sorely angered by the suggestion.

In a moment the victory banquet turned into a bloody contest between Christian and Muslim knights. Huon used his horn to summon Oberon, who, because Huon had already suffered so much for his earlier lie, obeyed the summons. With his help the Christian forces prevailed against the knights of Babylon. Huon decapitated Gaudys and was able to cut off his beard and pluck four teeth from his mouth to take back to Charlemagne.

After this great victory Huon set out on the long journey home with his companions and Claramond. When he reached Bordeaux, he was visited by Oberon, who reconciled Charlemagne and Huon and promised that at the end of four years, when he was called to Heaven, he would offer Huon his fairy kingdom if Huon would bequeath to Gerames his territories in Bordeaux. And when his adventuring days were over, Huon did indeed become King of the Fairies.

The Rebel Lords

Charlemagne assumes the role of wrathful tyrant in the colourful late twelfth-century French epic that recounts the adventures of the four sons of Duke Aymon: Aalard, Renaud, Guichard and Richard. These tales are an example of the "feudal cycle" of *chansons*, which deal with the exploits of barons drawn into conflict with the king.

Les Quatre Fils Aymon, or "The Four Sons of Aymon" (also known as "Renaud of Montauban"), was an extremely popular story and was translated into German, Italian, Scandinavian and English. The earliest manuscript is from the late twelfth century, but scholars believe that older versions may have been lost.

The four brothers were popular members of Charlemagne's circle. One day, however, the king's jealous nephew Bertolai picked a quarrel with Renaud and during the ensuing fight, the noble son of Aymon killed the impetuous youth. The four brothers at once fled the imperial court and took refuge in the Ardennes – in the poem an enchanted forest of uncertain location. Here they built the towering fortress of Montessor.

Aymon's four sons were tracked down by the furious Charlemagne, who laid siege to Montessor. The castle's occupants resisted until Hervieux de Lausanne, won over to the king's side, opened the gates. The brothers fled once more and for seven years survived in the French countryside as bandits. Then they travelled to the south of France with their cousin Maugis, a powerful sorcerer.

After helping King Yon of Gascony repel an invading Saracen army, Renaud built a new fortress, Montauban, and married Yon's fair sister, Clarisse.

But Charlemagne discovered the quartet once more and arrived at Montauban with his brave knight Roland. Maugis used his power of sorcery to disguise Renaud who, on his magnificent steed Bayard, beat Roland in a horse race. He then seized the ruler's crown and fled.

Yon later betrayed the brothers and a number of fierce battles ensued in which Maugis repeatedly came to the aid of his cousins. Then they again retreated to Montauban, where Charlemagne besieged them once more. They came close to starvation, and for a time their only nourishment was the blood of Renaud's horse Bayard.

The sons of Aymon eventually escaped via an underground passage and went to Tremoigne (modern Dortmund, Germany), where they captured Duke Richard of Normandy and used him as a hostage to bargain with Charlemagne for a truce.

Renaud next had many adventures while voyaging with Maugis to the Holy Land, where they helped Christian forces take Jerusalem from the Saracens. Back in France, Renaud settled with his family for some years before travelling as a penitent to Cologne. There he helped build the city's magnificent cathedral, but when he was in the nave one day stonemasons, angered by his exertions, turned on him and beat him to death. Bells tolled unrung, fish left the waters and many other portentous miracles were seen in the hour of Renaud's passing, and after his death he was revered as a saint.

Stories abounded in the Middle Ages of how knights such as Renaud would bleed their mounts for blood to slake their thirst. This horse is a detail from the 14th-century *Luttrell Psalter*.

The Tragedy of Raoul de Cambrai

The tale of a French knight, Raoul de Cambrai, dispossessed as a child of his inheritance by Charlemagne's son King Louis I, is one of the best-known episodes in the **Quatre Fils Aymon** *cycle.*

The Count de Cambrai died while his wife Aalais was pregnant with their son, Raoul. King Louis tried to force Aalais to marry Gibouin le Manceau, but she proudly declined. The furious Louis then seized Raoul's inheritance and gave it to Gibouin in perpetuity.

As he grew up, Raoul learned the skills of knighthood from his squire Bernier – and a taste for bitterness and revenge from his wicked uncle Guerri le Sor.

Raoul became a favoured member of court, but one day two young brothers were killed while under his supervision. Although Raoul was not to blame, he was too proud to explain and the boys' father, Ernaut de Douai, declared undying enmity.

Raoul pressed Louis to restore his inheritance, but the king refused. Raoul then declared he would seize the lands anyway, so Gibouin pleaded for the king's protection. As a palliative, Louis offered Raoul the lands of the next knight to die. Raoul accepted these terms, though they were highly unchivalrous.

Herbert de Vermandois soon died leaving four adult sons, one of them the father of Raoul's squire, Bernier. Raoul demanded that Louis keep his promise and the king assented but said that Raoul would have to win the land in battle.

Both Bernier and Aalais tried to dissuade Raoul from rendering unto another the wrong he had suffered himself. He would not listen, and after a fierce quarrel with his mother the proud Raoul rode fully armed into the Vermandois territories. He and his troops attacked and destroyed the Convent of Origny, despite the pleas for mercy of the Abbess Marsent who was Bernier's mother. Bernier himself then came to blows with Raoul but fled, hurt, to his father's camp. Then Raoul met his sworn enemy Ernaut de Douai, alongside Bernier, in battle. As the three fought Raoul declared that God Himself could not save Ernaut – a blasphemy that sealed his fate. Raoul was killed by Bernier and his body borne sorrowfully home.

Doomed Love

The adventures in battle and love of Roland, Oliver and Charlemagne's other leading paladins formed the basis of a new cycle of romance epics created in Italy in the fifteenth and sixteenth centuries. The details and the names sometimes changed with the authors, but the themes of love and warfare remained true to the demands of the chivalric code.

The first books of Matteo Maria Boiardo's *Orlando Innamorato* ("Roland In Love") were published in 1483 and combined the conflicts of the Charlemagne tradition with the amorous intrigues of the tales of King Arthur and his court.

At the start of the epic, knights gathered in their thousands in Paris to take part in a tournament at the Church festival of Pentecost. Into their midst rode the beautiful warrior-maiden Angelica, accompanied by her brother Argalia. They had come from the pagan court of their father Galafrone, King of Cathay (China).

Angelica announced that whoever could unhorse Argalia would win her hand and favours – an offer which was greeted excitedly by the knights of Charlemagne's court. Foremost among them was Orlando, who was drawn to Angelica like a moth to a flickering flame. He could not stop from feasting his eyes on her – although at his side was fair Alda (who, in this version of the tale, was his wife).

Argalia, however, wore magic armour and bore a golden lance that made him invincible – for he and his sister had come to lay low the knights of Charlemagne's court and prepare the way for an army led by Agramante, Emperor of Africa, and Gradasso, King of Sericana, a country in southeast Asia. He wanted to capture the sword of Orlando, here called Durindan, and possess his cousin Ranaldo's magnificent horse named, like Renaud's, Bayard.

The knights drew lots to determine the order in which they would fight, for all wanted to be first. The tourney was to be at Merlin's Stone, near the royal court, and under its rules once a knight was unseated he had to give up the contest. First to ride into combat was an English duke named

Astolfo who was defeated. Feraguto, a Spanish Muslim, rode next. He was also knocked down, but then he broke the rules by continuing the fight on foot. Argalia and Angelica then withdrew, but many knights including Orlando and Ranaldo, driven by desire for the fair maiden, followed them into the Forest of Arden. (This enchanted glade would pass into the works of William Shakespeare by way of the English playwright and author of prose romances, Thomas Lodge.)

There in a shady glade Ranaldo found a fountain which made sweet music as it splashed. He drank deeply, unaware that the magic waters had the power to extinguish the ardour of his heart and make him hate fair Angelica. As he straightened,

wiping his lips, he felt a surge of hatred for the lady. Then he came upon a twinkling stream, whose waters brought whoever tasted them into a passion of love – many knights in the long days of chivalry had been undone here. But Ranaldo was no longer thirsty and did not feel like drinking; so he lay down beneath the heavy branches of a towering tree and slept.

Angelica soon passed by and drank from the stream. Then she saw brave Ranaldo sleeping and she felt a surge of passion for his noble form. She gathered flowers and dropped the petals on his face. Waking to the sight of the lady he now scorned, he leaped onto his horse and rode away. Angelica threw herself onto the ground where he had slept and lay stricken with grief.

Elsewhere in the forest, Feraguto found Argalia and they fought bitterly on foot until Feraguto triumphed, stabbing the knight from Cathay in the groin. Argalia died and Feraguto cast his body into one of the many waterways that traversed the forest.

Orlando then found Angelica asleep on the ground. He was gazing on her beauty when he was interrupted by Feraguto, who challenged him to fight. They struggled back and forth across the glade but before either had triumphed Angelica awoke and fled upon her white palfrey. On the two knights fought until they were interrupted by another maiden, Fiordespina, who begged her cousin Feraguto to return to Spain, which was under attack by the Oriental army of King Gradasso. Feraguto left at once, while Orlando rode on in search of Angelica.

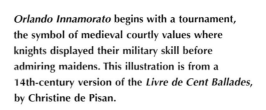

Orlando Innamorato begins with a tournament, the symbol of medieval courtly values where knights displayed their military skill before admiring maidens. This illustration is from a 14th-century version of the *Livre de Cent Ballades*, by Christine de Pisan.

After encounters with fierce giants and a sojourn in an enchanted garden where he forgot Angelica, Charlemagne and his love of honour, he came to Angelica's castle at Albraca – thought by scholars to be Bukhara in modern Uzbekistan. Here he confronted Emperor Agricane of Tartary (southern Russia and Siberia) who, unknown to Orlando, also loved Angelica. In the ensuing duel, Agricane lured his opponent into the desolate countryside, and they ended their conflict in a forest glade by a whispering fountain. When night fell, they rested and talked as gentle knights will, but when it emerged that both loved Angelica they leaped once more into the saddle and pursued their quarrel by moonlight. Dawn rose and still they fought, but finally Orlando prevailed. Before he expired, Agricane repented his pagan ways and begged Orlando to baptize him – and so at the nearby fountain Orlando opened for him the way to Paradise.

A 15th-century gold brooch with sword-like clasp. Christian knights like Orlando were as skilled in the arts of love as in the ways of war.

After many more adventures, Ranaldo, Orlando and Angelica all returned to France, where Charlemagne was threatened by King Rodamonte at the head of Agramante's heathen army. Ranaldo found his way once more to the magical Forest of Arden, but there in a meadow decked with flowers he was attacked by three naked maidens and their young lord. These four assaulted the knight with the flowers they carried which, by their magic, laid him low, giving him deep and dreadful pains in his bones. Then they departed, but one of the maidens returned and, explaining that the youth was the love god Cupid himself, told Ranaldo of a sweet stream that flowed through Arden that could soothe his aches.

He wandered slowly, limping as if after a great battle, until he found the stream, and there he drank deep. But it was the water that plunged knights and ladies headlong into love, and even as he raised his head he felt a pang of yearning for Angelica and at once forgot his hatred of her.

By this time Angelica had fallen in love with a knight called Radamont, but was travelling with Orlando through the forest. They came to a fountain and she dismounted from her palfrey to drink. But this one was Merlin's Fountain, which had the power to freeze even the most passionate heart, and as soon as she drank her love for Radamont left her. And then that very knight rode by.

Radamont, bemused by Angelica's cold reception, begged her forgiveness. This led him into a quarrel with her companion, whom he did not recognize – for Orlando was wearing an unfamiliar crest. They soon came to blows – but their mighty swords Durindan and Fusberta were no strangers to each other.

Angelica fled and soon came across Charlemagne's army pitching camp to face the Saracens. When she explained that Orlando was in the magic groves of Arden nearby, Charlemagne himself rode there, separated the knights and promised them that the one who fought most bravely against the pagans would win Angelica. He put the lady in the care of Duke Namo, and Orlando and Ranaldo returned with the royal army to Paris.

Boiardo's poem was unfinished when he died. It broke off with Charlemagne still under threat from the pagan armies. Angelica escaped from Duke Namo's camp and was pursued by Ranaldo, while at the Battle of Montalbano the pagan prince Ruggiero fell in love with the chaste warrior maiden Bradamante – their later union would, Boiardo said, give issue to his patrons, the Este family, rulers of Ferrara in northern Italy. The story was later continued by Lodovico Ariosto (1474–1533) in *Orlando Furioso* ("Roland Maddened"), first published in 1516, which prolonged the rivalry between Orlando and Ranaldo for the hand of fair Angelica. Ariosto, who like Boiardo enjoyed the patronage of the Este family, made much of the romance between Ruggiero and Bradamante (see box, opposite).

Bradamante and Ruggiero

In Orlando Furioso, Ranaldo's sister Bradamante, who rode as the Virgin Knight clad in white armour, won the heart of the pagan champion Ruggiero – but, as Ariosto's audience demanded, there were many twists and turns in their romance.

Ruggiero was said to be descended from Hector of Troy. Nursed in infancy by a lioness, he was a ward of the magician Atlas, who kept him away from harm because a prophecy had foretold his early death.

Bradamante freed Ruggiero from Atlas's castle, which was spun from spells – only for Atlas to sweep the hero away once more on a hippogryph, a winged horse with a griffin's head. He was then freed again by another knight and travelled far and wide, but Atlas always worked to bring him back to safety.

One enchanted day, deep in a forest glade, Ruggiero encountered a knight and a giant locked in single combat. The giant downed and prepared to dispatch his opponent, but just then the

knight's helmet came loose and Ruggiero saw that the fallen champion was none other than his beloved Bradamante. As he leaped forward to save her, the giant swept her up and ran deeper into the forest with the knight over his shoulder, leading Ruggiero to an enchanted castle. There he searched for her but without success, for Atlas had had his way once more: both the maiden in the likeness of Bradamante and the castle itself he had created by his magic.

The time came when the real Bradamante rode by the same glade and Atlas used a phantom in the comely shape

of Ruggiero to lure the virgin champion into his lair. She too searched vainly for her beloved. When they were later freed from the spell by the English paladin Astolfo, Bradamante and Ruggiero embraced passionately. The pagan knight declared his love and converted to the Christian faith to win her hand.

Eventually, the two were wed at Charlemagne's court; splendid pavilions were raised and the fields decorated with garlands.

The Song of El Cid

When the nobleman Don Rodrigo Diaz de Vivar died in 1099, the legend of the Spanish hero El Cid was born. Within half a century, the epic poem of his life, *Cantar de Mio Cid* ("Song of my Cid"), had been composed and countless ballads praising his deeds sung.

The legend was closely based on the life of the historical Don Rodrigo. Even during his lifetime this great general was known by his legendary name El Cid – derived from the Arabic *as-sid* ("lord") – and as El Campeador ("the Champion"). But many fanciful tales clustered around him and were duly recorded in the chronicle accounts which helped establish El Cid's heroic image, passing over some of the less savoury episodes in his colourful life.

Rodrigo was born in 1043 in Bivar near Burgos, and was raised at the court of King Ferdinand I of Castile and Leon under the protection of Sancho, the king's eldest son. On Ferdinand's death, Sancho ascended the throne and appointed the twenty-two-year-old Don Rodrigo *armiger regis* or commander of the royal troops. He filled the post with great distinction and earned the name El Campeador.

In 1072 Sancho was killed while fighting against his brother Alfonso, who had risen in revolt and soon after succeeded him. Don Rodrigo was accepted at court but was ousted as *armiger regis* by Count Garcia Ordonez. Thus began a bitter enmity between the two proud warriors.

El Cid's most prized possessions were his horse Bavieca and his powerful sword Tizona, shown here, which is kept today in his home town of Burgos.

In 1079 Don Rodrigo defeated and captured Ordonez after a military encounter during a visit to the king of Seville. His enemies at court were many and King Alfonso VI exiled him from Castile in 1081. While he was away from Castile, Don Rodrigo fought in the service of al-Mu'tamin, the Moorish king of Saragossa in northeastern Spain, inflicting a number of decisive defeats on Spanish rulers both Christian and Moorish.

As soon as King Alfonso VI found himself in trouble with the Moors, however, he recalled Don Rodrigo, who was still recognized as the greatest Christian general in Spain. But their reconciliation was short-lived and Don Rodrigo was exiled from Castile once more. From 1090 onwards Don Rodrigo's military efforts were directed to winning control of the powerful Moorish kingdom of Valencia. After a siege of many months he finally conquered the city in 1094.

El Cid inflicted two great defeats on Moorish armies in 1094 and 1096, but he died not long afterwards in Valencia on 10 July 1099. In 1101 the Muslims laid siege to the city. King Alfonso VI, arriving to defend it, decided that he could not hold it and burned it before abandoning it to the besiegers. El Cid's body was taken back to Castile and reburied at the monastery of San Pedro de Cardena, near his birthplace of Burgos.

First Honours

According to legend, Don Rodrigo first won a military reputation defending the honour of his father, Diego Laynez. Because Laynez was advancing in years he could not respond when Don Gomez insulted him, but instead took to grief-stricken solitude. Then Don Rodrigo challenged Don Gomez to conflict in the field and overcame him with a mighty sword's stroke, slicing his head from his shoulders and carrying it to Diego Laynez. Before many weeks had passed, Diego died with his pride restored, a happy man.

King Ferrando (Ferdinand I) was approached by Ximena, the daughter of Count Gomez, whom Don Rodrigo had humbled in death to avenge his father. She begged the king to give her away as wife to Don Rodrigo, for she was enamoured of his strength and abilities and willing to pardon him for her father's death. The king agreed, and Don Rodrigo was happy to acquiesce in the proposal for Ximena was beautiful indeed. The couple were wed amid great ceremony.

With Don Rodrigo, the king then embarked on a campaign against the Moorish kingdoms of southern Spain, capturing many cities. Everywhere Don Rodrigo won praise for his bravery and skill in battle. When they travelled on into the northern kingdom of Leon, five Moorish kings who were vassals of Don Rodrigo came to offer him tribute. The knight was never covetous of wealth, and so he offered the money to King Ferrando, but the monarch refused it as not rightfully his – and, having heard the Moors call Don Rodrigo "Cid", declared that this great and noble-spirited warrior should henceforth be known as El Cid.

At that time the Holy Roman Emperor, Henry III, complained to Pope Victor II that King Ferrando did not recognize the emperor's authority and send him tribute as he should, and the pope dispatched a message to the Spanish ruler threatening to launch a crusade against him if he did not give way on this matter. The king's advisers were inclined to bow to the pope's authority, but El Cid angrily declared that it was demeaning for such a glorious sovereign to pay tribute to any man. He therefore advised waging war against the Holy Roman Emperor.

The king marched to war, with El Cid leading the vanguard of the army. In the first battle El Cid defeated Remon, Count of Savoy, who offered up his beautiful daughter to the great general's care in return for his own freedom. Then he trounced a great French army. When King Ferrando and the main part of his forces caught up, they decided to dispatch El Cid and certain other nobles to the pope, requesting him to send a cardinal to draw up a covenant establishing that the emperor could not demand tribute from the Spanish king. The pope, advised of El Cid's invincibility in battle, aquiesced. Earlier, El Cid had handed Count Remon's fair daughter to King Ferrando, who made passionate love to her; their son was later summoned to Rome by the pope and in time achieved great honour as Cardinal Ferrando.

The Spanish countryside remains rich in reminders of the long struggle to reunite the country under Christian rule. One such site is the fortress of La Suda at Lleida (Lerida), in northeastern Spain, which was taken from the Moors in 1149.

El Cid was as noted for his cunning as for his bravery – a side of his character shown when he fooled the merchants by entrusting them with boxes filled with sand rather than money. This ivory chest is from Cuenca, *c.*1050.

El Cid is Exiled

When Sancho II was killed while leading an army against his brother, all Castilian subjects had to accept Alfonso VI as their new king. But just several years into Alfonso's reign El Cid was banished from his beloved Castile. Out of jealousy the Castilian nobles plotted against the great general, persuading their monarch that El Cid's actions in driving back a Moorish incursion to Toledo had not been warranted and were designed to disturb good relations with the Moorish king of the city. Taking their side, Alfonso banished El Cid – and he did not allow him the customary thirty days to quit his territories but instead commanded him to be gone in just nine.

It is with this episode that the *Cantar de Mio Cid* begins, although the first pages of the poem's sole surviving manuscript (*c.*1307) are lost and have had to be reconstructed. When leaving, El Cid looked back at his abandoned home with its echoing halls, bare porches and swinging doors, and was afflicted with great sadness, but he praised the Lord for the chances brought even by adversity. He reminded his men that the author of his misfortune was the king and not the honest people of Castile, and instructed them never to mistreat the poor while on their travels in exile.

In the city of Burgos, none of the citizens dared offer hospitality to El Cid and his men for fear of what the king would do to them in his fury; but they lamented openly that so great a noble should not have a lord worthy of him. Even the inn was closed to the company, and, after El Cid had said prayers in Santa Maria Cathedral, he was obliged to leave the city and camp with his men in the open countryside.

All the merchants of Burgos had refused to sell food and drink to the company – save one, Martin Antolinez, who was El Cid's nephew. He was happy to bring bread and wine to the warriors, and in doing so he approached his uncle and asked to become one of their company – for, he said, if he stayed in the city the king would punish him for what he had done.

Then El Cid, complaining that he had no way of raising money, devised a cunning plan with which Martin was happy to help. They took chests and filled them with sand. Then Martin found two merchants and persuaded them that the chests were filled with treasure won in El Cid's campaigns against the Moors. He claimed that since the boxes were too heavy for El Cid to carry with him into exile, he was willing to leave them in their care in return for a reasonable sum of money as surety for them – but they must swear never to look inside the chests for a whole year.

The merchants were taken in and agreed to advance 600 marks against the treasure. They came to El Cid's camp, where they found that the chests were too heavy for them to lift – a discovery that gave them great delight. Martin helped the merchants drag the coffers to a safe place in the city and the deal was concluded with a gift of thirty marks to Martin for his role as go-between. The chests that El Cid filled with sand were said to have been preserved after his death and supposedly hang in two churches – one in the church of Santa Agueda at Burgos and the other in the monastery of San Pedro de Cardena.

El Cid and the Leper

El Cid's generosity towards a roadside beggar is typical of many legendary episodes celebrating Don Rodrigo's piety and knightly virtue preserved in late medieval Spanish ballads and chronicles.

The great El Cid rode at the head of a company of twenty knights, to pay his respects at the shrine of James, Spain's national saint, at Santiago de Compostela.

Wherever the path of the pilgrimage took him he showed generosity to the beggars that crowded near. Then he came upon a leper in the road, calling in a frail voice for Christian charity. Many a man would have ridden by, giving the wretch a wide berth, but El Cid stopped his horse, dismounted and helped the leper to his feet. With no fear that he would be contaminated by the terrible disease, he helped the man into the saddle, then climbed up himself and rode on with the leper sharing his mount.

When they came to an inn, Don Rodrigo insisted that the leper also be admitted and even brought him to his own table to eat.

As the candles were lit at the end of the day Don Rodrigo led the leper into the chamber he himself had been allocated and there allowed him to share his bed.

In the darkest hour of midnight the Christian warrior woke with a start, feeling a cold breath between his shoulders. He leaped from his bed and called for a light; when the shadows were banished neither he nor the manservant could see the leper anywhere in the chamber.

Then the great champion of many a battlefield fell to his knees, for he saw an apparition blazing with the light of Heaven. The ghost spoke with a flesh-and-blood voice, declaring itself to be Lazarus, the corpse raised from death by Christ himself. He, Lazarus, had taken the form of the leper whose suffering El Cid had relieved the previous day. Then he praised El Cid's battlefield prowess and foretold a wonderful future for the warrior, with victories over Muslim and Christian enemies alike, an honourable death and welcome into Paradise. The vision faded, and for the rest of the night Don Rodrigo remained on his knees praising the Virgin Mary and God the Father, Son and Holy Ghost.

Then El Cid broke camp and said a prayer to the Blessed Virgin Mary. Before he left Burgos he pledged that when he had the money he would pay for 1,000 masses in the cathedral of Santa Maria there. Then he rode through the night, arriving at daybreak at the monastery of San Pedro de Cardena, where his wife Dona Ximena and his daughters were taking refuge. There was great joy when El Cid made his presence known. He gave money to Abbot Sisebuto, for the care of his family and tarried with them, enjoying their company, however briefly.

Later that same day, 115 chivalrous knights from Castile came to the monastery in the company of Martin Antolinez and in search of El Cid, declaring their desire to follow him into exile – and he came out and greeted them warmly. Early the next morning, after a blessing from Abbot Sisebuto and a tender parting from El Cid's beloved daughters and wife, the knights left. The *Cantar de Mio Cid* describes how Dona Ximena offered a long and devout prayer to the glory of God, asking the Almighty to keep El Cid safe and bring wife and husband back together some happier day in the future.

Along the road more knights came to join up with the exile until he had a company of fully 300 mounted warriors accompanied by foot soldiers.

On his last night before quitting Castile El Cid was visited in his dreams by the Archangel Gabriel himself, who promised him glory in battle, success in life and a comfortable old age.

Rich Pickings

In the Moorish kingdom of Toledo, El Cid surprised and captured the rich city of Castejon. He shared the booty among his men and sold his portion to local Moorish peoples for a great sum. Then he sent messages to Alfonso, saying that even in exile there was work he could do for his monarch among the Moors.

El Cid and his men moved on, plundering as they went, until they came to the city of Alcocer. For fifteen weeks they lay in wait outside the town until the general ordered his men to break camp and ride away as if they had abandoned the siege. The people of Alcocer poured out in pursuit, and El Cid told his knights and soldiers to increase their speed as if they were fleeing in fear. When he had drawn the people a good distance from the gates, he gave the signal for his army to turn. They swept back towards the city, overrunning their enemy and taking control of the prize. Magnanimous in victory, the general spared the lives of the Moors he had taken prisoner.

Then the Moorish king of Valencia sent a great army to attack Alcocer, and it settled in for a siege. When it had invested the walls for four weeks, El Cid resolved to break out and attack the Moors, even though his troops were grievously outnumbered. They readied themselves for battle and El Cid gave his banner to a knight named Pedro Bermudez, who was greatly honoured.

The next morning they rode out bravely; the Moors were taken by surprise but at once beat their heavy drums of war so loudly that the Earth itself seemed to shake. El Cid held his knights back. Pedro Bermudez impetuously dashed forward with the banner and rode right into the heart of the Moorish horsemen. Then the Moors set upon him, but he fought with great steadfastness and despite the countless soldiers teeming around him, they still could not capture the banner.

Seeing this, El Cid spurred his great horse forward with his knights following and every one of them brought his opposite number low in the first charge. The Christian knights fought heroically that day, making light of the fact that they were outnumbered, driving the besiegers to flight. The chroniclers recount that by the battle's end 1,300 Moors lay slain on the field while only fifteen Christians had been killed. El Cid, as ever, shared out the spoils of battle with great fairness.

For three years he rampaged through the Moorish kingdoms of Spain. His reputation went before him and he made great profit in exacting tribute from the Moorish rulers there. He sent much of the money to the cathedral in Burgos, and to keep his wife, children and Abbot Sisebuto in comfort at San Pedro Cardena.

Valencia Captured

When he sent out a proclamation that he intended to attack the city of Valencia, many Christian knights were attracted by the promise of plunder and joined him. El Cid's forces besieged Valencia for nine months until the city surrendered. Once his banner flew over Valencia, Don Rodrigo and his men had more wealth than they had ever seen.

El Cid established Christian rule in Valencia and ordained a bishop, Don Jerome, for the city. Then out of the great wealth that he had taken on capturing the city, he sent another gift by way of Minaya Alvar Fanez to King Alfonso VI: 100 stallions girded for war, with the message that he still regarded himself as Alfonso's vassal. He humbly requested that the king allow his wife and daughters to join him in Valencia. He also sent full payment to the gullible merchants in Burgos.

Alfonso VI was pleased with the gift and assented to El Cid's request. Minaya Alvar Fanez brought great joy to the monastery at San Pedro with the news that Dona Ximena and her daughters were free to join El Campeador in Valencia. Escorted by many knights, the ladies rode in safety as far as the plain before the city, where El Cid came out to meet them on his magnificent mount Bavieca (see box, page 55). He wept with joy to be reunited with his beloved family after so long a separation.

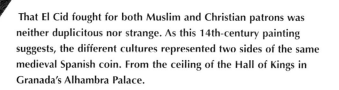

That El Cid fought for both Muslim and Christian patrons was neither duplicitous nor strange. As this 14th-century painting suggests, the different cultures represented two sides of the same medieval Spanish coin. From the ceiling of the Hall of Kings in Granada's Alhambra Palace.

The Death of El Cid

So successful was El Cid in quelling rebellions that Spain entered a period of peace during which the great general lived quietly in Valencia. But he was to be called on to fight for Spain once more – only this time he knew it would be his last campaign.

The legend has it that Don Rodrigo, after repelling a number of Moorish attacks on Valencia, lived in great peace within the city he had won for himself, resorting to arms only to quell any internal revolts. After five years, however, word came that King Bucar of Morocco was approaching its walls with an army vast beyond reckoning.

Seeing that a great conflict was inevitable, El Cid sent the Moorish inhabitants out of the city so they would not become embroiled in the battle. Then, that night, Don Rodrigo was visited by St Peter himself. The saint informed El Cid that it now pleased God to call his warrior to Heaven. At the end of thirty days El Cid would pass away and, leaving his body on Earth, would ascend to Paradise. He should not worry, however, for his army would win the impending battle against King Bucar even without him; before he died he should instruct his lieutenants in the matter and show them how to mount his corpse on Bavieca so that he could lead his troops to victory even after death. The following day El Cid wept as he told his knights that the time had come for him to leave this world behind.

On the eighth day, El Cid preached a great sermon, confessed his sins and then took to his bed, where he lay for the last seven days of his life. He ate and drank nothing but a mixture of rose water and myrrh, with some balsam sent as a gift from a Persian ruler. Day by day he grew weaker, but his skin became clearer and fresher.

On the day before his death he called to him Dona Ximena, Gil Diaz, Minaya Alvar Fanez and other leading nobles and gave them instructions on what to do following his death, just as St Peter had commanded. He then told them that after the battle they should leave the city forever and return to Castile. Then he passed peacefully away.

His followers mournfully carried out his commands. In the early hours of the thirteenth day after his death, they rode out against King Bucar's vast army. Gil Diaz propped his master's corpse upright on two boards attached to the saddle so that it could not fall. El Cid's skin was fresh and sweet-smelling, as if he lived still. The knights then formed up behind Bavieca.

The monastery of San Pedro de Cardena, ten kilometres south of Burgos, where, according to legend, El Cid's body sat on a throne for ten years before burial without decaying. Earlier in his life the general and his family took refuge here on their way to exile after being expelled from Castile by King Alfonso VI.

Bavieca: A Steed Fit for a Hero

El Campeador's magnificent steed Bavieca, which carried its master even after the great warrior was dead, is celebrated in the El Cid ballads as Don Rodrigo's companion and his equal in strength and gallantry.

According to the *Cantar de Mio Cid*, Don Rodrigo captured Bavieca relatively late in his career from an unnamed king of Seville, who had tried to recapture Valencia after El Cid had occupied the city. El Cid rode Bavieca for the first time when he went out to greet Dona Ximena and his daughters. All writers agree that the horse was powerful and fearlessly loyal. One ballad celebrates El Cid's mastery as a rider and Bavieca's obedience as a horse. Once as Don Rodrigo put the horse through its paces before King Alfonso VI, the reins broke but El Cid was not thrown and brought Bavieca safely home. Then he offered Alfonso the horse as a gift, but the king respectfully refused the proposal.

By tradition, Bavieca was never ridden by another man after El Cid died. At the monastery of San Pedro, El Cid's loyal companion Gil Diaz mated Bavieca with two of the finest mares he could find, and for long afterwards the best horses in Castile were said to be descended from Bavieca.

Tradition also has it that Bavieca died, aged forty, two-and-a-half years after his master. He was buried opposite the gate of the monastery and Gil Diaz planted two elm trees over the grave. Bavieca's strength in life must have had issue in death, for these two trees grew to a great height and were blessed with a glorious and abundant foliage.

Statue of El Cid on his trusty horse Bavieca, in the centre of his home town of Burgos, the capital of Castile. In his hand he holds his famous sword, Tizona.

Never was there such a victory as that won by the Christians against King Bucar's hordes. Chroniclers say that the ranks of El Cid's force were swelled by a heavenly army of fully 70,000 mounted men, led by a knight brandishing a bloody Cross and a sword of fire. The Moorish troops fled, but the Christians pursued them even into the sea. Ten thousand were killed in the waves, which boiled blood red.

The Christians gathered riches beyond imagining in battle spoils and began the long victorious ride back to Castile. Still El Cid sat upright in his saddle, now dressed as a nobleman would be for such a journey – and still his body showed no signs of physical decay.

At the monastery of San Pedro de Cardena, they held a great funeral but they did not bury his body. Instead they dressed it in fine clothes. Placing the dead leader's trusty sword Tizona in his hand, they set the corpse majestically on an ivory chair to the right of the altar of St Peter.

It was a signal of El Cid's great holiness that his body did not decay and retained its sweet fragrance – traditionally in the Catholic Church these were attributes of a saint's corpse. For ten years El Cid's body rested in that ivory chair and did not rot. After that time it was respectfully moved into a vault. When, four years after Don Rodrigo's death, his devoted Dona Ximena also died she was buried at the foot of the chair.

55

A Chivalric Alexander

The exploits of the fourth-century BC
Macedonian general Alexander the Great,
conqueror of the Persian empire and of
northern India, were the basis of a series
of romance narratives that were familiar
from the Indian Ocean to northern Europe
throughout the medieval era.

Alexander's magnificent achievements inspired
colourful folklore in the years immediately after his
death in 323BC. The first to write a history of him
was a man from Alexandria named Cleitarchus.
In AD300 a series of fanciful Alexander narratives
were written in Greek; these were supposedly by
one of Alexander's generals, Callisthenes, and the
text is therefore known to scholars as the Pseudo-
Callisthenes. It contains a series of letters said to
have been written by Alexander to his tutor,
Aristotle, and his mother Olympias.

Translations were made into Latin, Armenian
and Pahlavi but it was not until the writers of
medieval romance started to claim Alexander as
one of their own heroes that his image began to
flourish in the minds of Western audiences whose
imaginations had been primed by exotic tales of
the East spun by veterans of the crusades.

According to a version of the romance written
around 1100 by the French writer Alberic, many
auspicious portents marked the day of Alexander's
birth. The earth gaped and the sky grew dark,
while at sea the waves whipped themselves into a
frenzy; then lightning cracked the heavens and
blood-red waters fell as rain. But the moment
Alexander was born, all became calm.

He grew fast, a delightful child but preco-
cious in his abilities. His father Philip, it was
claimed, appointed great men, including Homer,
Ptolemy and Aristotle, to be the boy's tutors. They
taught him Latin and the liberal arts but did not
neglect his physical education – Alexander learned

**This painting of Alexander, c.1550, shows how the conquering
hero of classical Greek history becomes the refined and gentle
knight of chivalric legend. The symbols of war remain, in his
armour, sword and the troops encamped behind him, but more
feminine sensibilities are suggested by the flowing locks, stylized
pose and the cupids at his feet.**

to hunt and to disport himself as a knight. He was also instructed in singing and playing the harp and the tambour, a small drum. But the tutors' greatest gift to Alexander was the capacity to distinguish between good and evil. These were all attributes any medieval warrior would respect.

Alexander Conquers the Heavens

Now Philip kept two mighty gryphons, the magnificent lions with eagles' heads and wings that are celebrated in Greek mythology. Once, deep in the countryside, young Alexander was proving his mettle as a huntsman when he was seized by the desire to harness and fly these beasts. He commanded a squire to lock them up and starve them for two days so that on the third he would be able to bend them to his will with the promise of food.

Alexander had a chair made and fitted a canopy to protect him when he flew near the sun. Then he strapped the chair to the gryphons and clambered on. In his hands he held long spits which held meat just out of reach of the two lion-birds. As they strained upwards to reach the meat, the beasts flapped their wings and bore Alexander to the skies.

Alexander flew so high that the courtiers lost sight of him. At that altitude the searing heat of the sun singed the wings of the gryphons, who plunged downwards to cooler air. Alexander decided to return to solid land and brought the gryphons safely down in a rich meadow in his father's realm. Philip was angry and reprimanded his son when Alexander returned to court, but Olympias, his devoted mother, wept tears of joy and clasped the future hero to her breast.

At the Edge of the World

Alexander's conquests took him to the limits of the known world. According to one legend, he journeyed to a mysterious realm which was shrouded in darkness. Leaving the bulk of his army in a well-fortified place, he selected 100 youths and some divisions of footsoldiers to go ahead with him.

Before long they came to a place where a bright fountain cascaded out of the gloom and an intoxicating fragrance hung in the air. Here Alexander ordered a break and asked his cook, Andreas, to prepare a meal. This man selected a dried fish but when he washed it in the fountain it suddenly came back to life, flipping and jumping in his hands. Andreas realized the waters had the power to give life to whatever touched them. Telling no one of his discovery, he collected a sample in a silver container.

After eating, Alexander and his soldiers pressed on. They came to another place bathed in light and here Alexander saw two birds with human faces. One spoke to him, warning him that he and his men were trespassing on the territory of the gods, and advised him to retreat with all haste. Even the fearless Alexander was frightened, but his attention was seized by the other bird, which foretold great military glory for the general if he led his army to the east. Then it disappeared with its companion into thin air.

Thrilling with excitement, Alexander called on his men to retrace their steps until they regained the light of the sun. But he told them they could gather whatever rock or stone they pleased as a memento of this strange adventure. Some thought the idea foolish and left well alone, but others did as he suggested. When the soldiers came back to daylight they found that the stones they had brought with them were in fact hunks of gold and other precious metals.

On the return to the main camp, Andreas used the marvellous waters of life he had collected to seduce the daughter of one of Alexander's concubines. When it emerged that Andreas had discovered the secret without telling anyone, Alexander was greatly angered. The general banished the young woman, now immortal, to live as a goddess of streams and waterfalls, then ordered Andreas to be cast into the ocean where he became a sea god, quick to anger.

Another story relates how, on one occasion, Alexander came to the land of the Amazons. These fierce women lopped off one breast to enable

Some of the stories about Alexander that filtered back from the Levant told of strange events, such as the tale explaining his attempt to fly by attaching gryphons to a chair. This picture shows the conqueror being lowered to the seabed in a glass cage where the fish crowd round him and pay him homage.

them to fire their arrows more effectively, but even warriors such as they agreed to pay tribute to him.

A further legend describes an adventure Alexander had when he led a great army into India. As he advanced, he received a message from a group of sages. They said they had heard of his approach but did not fear him – for he could pillage nothing in their village, where the only valued property was knowledge. Alexander then ordered his army to set up camp and approached the holy men with a small group of intimates. They were happy to talk to him and he questioned the wisest of them closely.

They taught him that life was stronger than death just as the sun was mightier than darkness. When men and women died, darkness covered them for a time – but life would rise within them again like a new dawn. The sages also told Alexander that his thirst for power and hunger for conquest would bring him nothing that would last for, like all men, he would die and others would take what he had won for themselves. Alexander spoke with the learned men of India for many hours, taking great pleasure in their discourse, and he found himself admitting that he wished for a rest from his endless campaigns of war.

The Poison Princess

In the first half of the fourteenth century Alexander was celebrated again in the *Gesta Romanorum* ("Deeds of the Romans"), a collection of stories featuring heroes of the classical era that each ended with a moral. Scholars believe they were written by Christian monks with a view to adding colour to sermons in monasteries.

One of these tales described how Alexander almost lost his life to a great beauty. The Queen of the North had raised her daughter on the foulest poisons, and in time the girl herself became poisonous. The queen, hearing of Alexander's great glory, sent her daughter to him to bring him low. The beautiful young woman made all men mad with desire, and when Alexander saw her he was ready to give anything to make her his wife. But Aristotle saw the truth and he warned Alexander that she was dangerous. Let them bring a criminal forward, some man who had been condemned to death, and allow him to dally with the princess, Aristotle suggested; then they would see what effect she truly had on mortal men.

Alexander agreed and watched with horror as the man fell gasping to the ground after a single brush of his lips against the maiden's cheek. He embraced his tutor and speedily dispatched the princess back to her mother's kingdom. The moral of the story was that Alexander represented a good Christian soul tempted by lust and the sins of the flesh, while Aristotle, who warned and saved him from a painful death, was the inner conscience that instructs the individual to avoid the pleasures of the body for the good of the soul.

Alexander's Letters to Aristotle

Some of the more exotic stories of the **Alexander Romance** *take the form of letters written by the young general to his tutor Aristotle and to his mother Olympias.*

One of Alexander's missives to Aristotle describes how, on a visit to an untamed part of the world, the general's army saw a great city that seemed to float in the air – for it was constructed on top of reeds that thronged a riverbank. When they tasted the river water it was foul, and some of the men who tried to bathe there were eaten by reptiles.

Later, when they were desperate with thirst after a long march, they came across a lake with sweet waters and camped beside it. That night, beneath the light of the moon, horned snakes and scorpions the length of a man's forearm emerged from the ground and attacked many of the soldiers. Fierce beasts came from nearby forests to drink at the lake; they included foul-breathed animals with the faces of women but the jaws and fangs of dogs.

On another campaign in India, Alexander was shown a sacred garden filled with talking trees. They stood at the centre of the garden, surrounded by a hedge. One, sacred to a sun god named Mitora, spoke three times each day – at dawn, noon and dusk; another, the tree of a moon god called Mayosa, spoke twice, at midnight and in the early morning. Alexander persuaded a priest to allow him access to the sacred precinct, and there at sunset he was astounded to hear

words actually emerge from the first tree. It made its utterance in the local language, and Alexander had to pester the priest to reveal what the oracle had said. In fact, it had warned Alexander that he would soon be killed by his own men.

Later that night he returned to the precinct close to the time when the moon tree was due to pronounce, and again he was

not disappointed. A cool breeze caressed the grove as a deep voice sounded from the timber, revealing more dread news – great Alexander would die at Babylon, far from home. In truth the gods spoke wisely for he was to face a mutiny that would force him to retreat from India and in 323BC at Babylon on the Euphrates Alexander would die – of fever, rather than treachery.

Richard the Lionheart

Fifty years after his death in 1199, King Richard I of England had become established as a hero of legend, a great knight who won glory for Christendom and humbled the Saracens in the Holy Land.

The earliest known Richard narrative is an Anglo-Norman romance, written before 1250. Although it is now lost, it appears to have served as the basis for a late thirteenth-century English poem about this fearless king, the epitome of knightly virtue.

Richard forged an international reputation as a daring commander during the Third Crusade (1189–92), when he came up against another charismatic general in the shape of the Saracen leader Saladin. Like Richard, Saladin was a figure both historical and legendary: the legend gilded the biography of Salah ed-din Yussuf ibn Ayub (1137–93), sultan of Egypt and Syria. A popular episode in the romances described an imaginary dual between the two rulers.

The poets told how in a dream Richard was warned by an angel that Saladin was carefully planning a devious trick. The Muslim leader had given Richard a magnificent horse to ride in their duel; but the angel revealed that the horse was no ordinary colt – it was the son of the mare Saladin intended to use. When the mare whinnied the colt would kneel down in an attempt to feed on its mother's milk, and Richard would be at the mercy of his cunning opponent. Richard therefore plugged the horse's ears with wax, so that however much Saladin's mare whinnied it had no effect. The English king also placed a broad beam across his mount's shoulders that enabled him to cut a wide swathe through the Muslim troops that surrounded them. Saladin was humbled in the encounter but he escaped with his life.

Richard's victory over Saladin is celebrated on these earthenware tiles, *c.*1255. Richard, on the left, can be identified by the lions on his shield. The wounded Saladin is about to fall.

The Old Man of the Mountains

Richard also became associated with colourful legends that grew up around the mysterious figure of Rashid ad-Din, otherwise known as the "Old Man of the Mountains" – the leader of the legendary Assassins. An elderly man, he is said to have built a walled garden of great beauty in which he planted fragrant herbs and created streams of milk and honey and which he peopled with angelic maidens and boys dressed in gold. He lured passing knights into this garden and they were so captivated by it that they believed themselves to be in Paradise already. He was able to make them do as he wished, for he promised that if they died on any mission he gave them, they would be rewarded by being admitted to the beautiful grove.

One such mission was the murder in April 1192 of Conrad, King of Jerusalem, an Italian, by two assassins disguised as monks. Some said it had been carried out at Richard's behest, but a letter from the Old Man of the Mountains claimed responsibility and cleared Richard of involvement. The note, however, was almost certainly forged. One English chronicle has it that the French king, Philip, sent a group of assassins to do away with Richard at Chinon in 1195, but failed.

The Lion's Heart

English, French, Italian and German crusaders were not a united front and often bickered ferociously. On his way home from the Third Crusade, Richard was captured and imprisoned by Leopold, Duke of Austria, and then by the Holy Roman Emperor Henry VI. Legends grew around this episode, as well as around Richard's death – he was struck by a bolt from a crossbow while besieging the castle of Chalus in France. The celebrated tale of how Richard came by his name Coeur de Lion ("Lionheart") was another popular story. The late thirteenth-century Middle English romance had Richard imprisoned by King Modard of Germany. While in his power he killed the king's son and seduced the king's daughter. An enraged Modard ordered that a starving lion be released

Durenstein Castle stands high above the River Danube in the Wachau Hills of Austria. Richard was held to ransom here after he was captured returning from the crusades.

in Richard's cell. Richard, however, was warned by the princess and, with no weapon to defend himself but his courage, he took forty silk handkerchiefs that she had given him and wound them around his arm for protection. When the lion approached he plunged his hand down the beast's throat, tore its heart from its breast and burst from his cell holding the bloody organ. In the banqueting hall he confronted Modard, dipped the heart in salt and spices and ate it with relish. Modard, in awe, named him Coeur de Lion.

The legends of Richard's death recount how he was wounded by a crossbow bolt in the head but fought on until he had taken the castle he was besieging. Before he died, the king found time to pardon the man who had killed him. Richard had committed many sins of passion and battlefield ardour in his life, and his soul did not fly directly to Heaven. God granted a vision to St Edmund of Abingdon (1175–1240) in which it was revealed that Richard spent thirty-three years in purgatory before being called to Paradise in March 1232.

Seven Champions of Christendom

In one late sixteenth-century English prose romance, seven chivalrous saints do battle in the name of Christ. They ride forth into bruising conflict with Saracen armies, necromancers and giants – as well as dragons and other monstrous beasts.

The Famous History of the Seven Champions of Christendom was written in 1596 by an Englishman, Richard Johnson, and celebrates the legendary achievements of the patron saints of England, Wales, Ireland, Scotland, France, Italy and Spain. Drawing on a rich tradition that stretched back several centuries, it is a prime example of the popularity of "chapbook" romances – so called because "chapmen" or itinerant traders peddled them in markets.

According to the romance, George was the son of the high steward of England, born after his mother dreamed that she had conceived a dragon. He emerged into the world with an image of just such a fearsome beast on his chest, on his hand was a cross as red as blood.

As an infant he was stolen by a wild lady of the woods named Kalyb, who raised him to become a sturdy youth.

When he came to manhood, she told him of his noble parentage and showed him a castle deep in a magic forest where she had enchanted and imprisoned six great Christian knights, all saints: Denis of France, James of Spain, Anthony of Italy, Andrew of Scotland, Patrick of Ireland and David of Wales. She declared that he would be the seventh of their number, St George of England, and that his reputation would spread throughout the world. Kalyb also gave George a suit of armour

made from Libyan steel that reflected the light of Heaven, a steed – like Renaud's named Bayard – and a sword, Ascalon, made by the Cyclops, the god Zeus's smiths in Greek mythology.

George worked Kalyb's magic against her and trapped her in a rock. Then he freed the six saints and they embarked upon their several adventures. George travelled to Egypt, where he slew a great dragon with silver scales and a golden belly that had been terrorizing the country and feasting upon the blood of maidens. He saved from certain death the dragon's next intended victim – King Ptolemy's fair daughter Sabra, whose beauty was compared to that of the Roman goddess of love, Venus. When Sabra fell for her saviour it enraged King Almidor of Morocco, a visitor to the court who longed to make the princess his wife.

Almidor plotted against George and convinced King Ptolemy that he was a danger. So Ptolemy sent George as messenger to the Sultan of Persia, with a letter asking the ruler to put the bearer to death as an enemy of Islam. Arriving at the sultan's court, George was thrown into jail. On the day appointed for his execution, two lions were sent into his cell, but he thrust his arms down their throats and tore their hearts out. In this he bettered even the performance of King Richard the Lionheart. The sultan, amazed, no longer desired to put George to death. But he cast him in a deep dungeon and there he languished, comforted only by his faith in God, for seven long years.

In time he escaped and rescued Sabra from Almidor. He was then reunited with the other champions, sending them to Persia to claim revenge. They defeated the pagan hosts in a bloody five-day battle that stained the parched land red. But the fiendish Persian necromancer

Christianity was the driving force behind the tales of chivalry and some of the greatest stories were those of Europe's patron saints. This Cross is from Ireland and dates from around 1120.

Osmond conjured up spirits in the form of fair damsels who then enticed the six great saints to turn their backs on their vows of chastity and follow them into a magical pavilion filled with rare comforts that Osmond had created from thin air.

St George, who had been with Sabra in Egypt, arrived in Persia on the day the six saints were led astray. When George came to the pavilion where they lay in sensual abandon, he was himself almost seduced by the alluring maidens. But he stiffened his resolve and tore down the tent, exposing it as the stuff of magic. He captured Osmond and chained him to a tree; the necromancer later tore himself to pieces in a frenzy.

George called the six champions to arms once more and they all fought and triumphed in a final battle for control of Persia, killing 200,000 pagans. St George became ruler of Persia and the six other champions became his dependent kings. Then they marched homewards towards Christian lands, making many converts to the True Faith as they went on their way.

Called To God

Time was one enemy the Champions of Christendom were unable to vanquish: all at last were overcome by age and had to retire from the pursuit of knightly renown. Each returned to his homeland and there offered penance for past sins before giving up his soul to Heaven.

Saint George and the Dragon, by Paolo Uccello (1397–1475).
One of the most enduring myths of the warrior-saints, the story of George rescuing the maiden from her reptilian kidnapper is often read as the symbolic victory of Christianity over paganism.

MAIDENS, MYSTERIES AND TRIALS OF LOVE

The biographer of Liutberg, a psalm-singing female hermit who lived in the early ninth century, declared that, "She would have been capable of learning if the weakness of her sex had not hindered her." Less than 100 years later, however, Germany's first woman poet, the noble Roswitha, responded: "May feminine weakness triumph and masculine power be defeated."

The Middle Ages saw the emergence of women not only as artists – such as the book illuminator, En of Tavara, the composer, Hildegard of Bingen, and the writers Marie de France and Christine de Pisan – but also as influential patrons, most particularly Eleanor of Aquitaine and her daughter, Marie de Champagne, who actively promoted the literary output of the philosophy known as *amour courtois* or courtly love. The stories and songs of the time also began to exalt women, although their idealized images tended still to reflect only society's well-born. And in a world where men were portrayed as paragons of chivalric action and judged by their behaviour towards women as much as by their courage, women were seen as passive, untouchable, deserving of eternal love and duty, even if they were other men's wives.

The reality, of course, was different, especially for non-first-born sons, who had to find themselves rich heiresses as a matter of survival. But even in the real world there existed knights such as Ulrich of Lichtenstein, who drank his beloved's bathwater and cut off a finger to prove his love.

The world pictured in romances was a place of love, magic, disguises and bold rescues. But while the heroines in the Constance cycle, for example, remained paragons of duty courted by men eager for an easy life, medieval literature was not one-dimensional. The Church was responsible for recording – and thereby influencing – much of the work; but in fact, a considerable amount of the output reflected very varied contemporary attitudes and was remarkable for the independent spirit of its female characters and the complex interactions between the sexes. Erec and Enide, for example, learned to balance their interests to further their romance, while many of the women depicted by Boccaccio and Marie de France, among others, were liberated and self-assured free-thinkers.

Opposite: **Illustration from Pierre Sala's book** *Maids and Winged Hearts, c.1500,* **a collection of love poems. The imagery alludes to the constantly sought but ever-elusive nature of true and everlasting love.**

Below: **Late 15th-century Franco-Flemish ivory comb. The carving shows musicians playing while male suitors court eligible women.**

A Worthy Knight's Prize

Stories of exemplary knightly conduct, often located in a mythic past borrowed from the legends of King Arthur and his court, delighted audiences in the twelfth and thirteenth centuries. Women were not merely the prizes for acts of valour but the motivating force behind them; a gallant's deeds were dedicated to increasing his beloved's glory.

The tale of Erec and Enide, written some time around 1170 by Chretien de Troyes, is the oldest Arthurian romance to have survived in any language. But although its author was one of the most influential of all Romance poets, hardly anything is known about him. He probably lived at Troyes, in northeast France, between 1160 and 1172, possibly as a herald-at-arms. His patroness for at least part of this time was Marie, Countess of Champagne, the daughter of Eleanor of Aquitaine. Eleanor grew up in a court that was the home of the troubadours who, in the early twelfth century, had begun to evolve a rich tradition of songs and stories about courtly love and chivalrous behaviour. Marie inherited her mother's tastes and aimed to make her court into what has been described as "a social experiment station, where these Provencal ideals of a perfect society were planted afresh".

A Tale of Honour and Duty

The troubadours sang about the inviolable links between love, honour and duty, and this is also the theme explored in Chretien's version of the story of Erec and Enide. Although Erec was a knight at Arthur's court, he was also the eldest son of a king called Lac. One day, Erec was out riding with Queen Guinevere and a handmaiden when they saw in the distance a powerful knight, accompanied by a beautiful damsel and a hideous dwarf. The queen wanted to know the stranger's name, but whenever anyone tried to approach him, the dwarf rushed forwards to drive them off with a leather whip and a barrage of insults. Erec was appalled at this unseemly behaviour, but because he had ridden out without his lance and armour he

was unable to challenge the mysterious nobleman. Determined that the knight should not go unpunished, however, Erec decided to follow him in the hope that they would pass some town where he might be able to hire suitable weapons.

Sure enough, the knight and his entourage soon came to a bustling city whose people were busy preparing for a fete to be held the next day. Despite the crowds, Erec found lodgings at the home of a poor old man. When the daughter of the house, who was called Enide, emerged to stable his horse, Erec could not believe his eyes: although she was dressed in a patched and ragged tunic, she was the most beautiful woman that he had ever seen. He was determined to have her as his wife and in the course of that very evening began looking for ways to win her.

Over supper, his host explained that he and Enide, despite their poverty, were related to the local count, and that many nobles had offered Enide sumptuous clothes and other gifts if she would marry them. None of them, said the old man, was good enough.

Erec, who had been trying his hardest to keep from staring at the beautiful young girl all night, was all ears, and when the conversation turned to the forthcoming fete, he saw his opportunity. The old man told Erec that each year a sparrowhawk was tied to a silver perch, and any knight who wished could send his mistress to claim it as her prize for being the loveliest woman present. If another knight disputed the claim, he was obliged to fight her champion. It happened that the man Erec was following had won bloody victories in the last two years, and nobody in the town expected a challenger to come forward this time.

But when the old man had finished Erec stood up and humbly asked if he could take Enide to win the hawk. Her father happily agreed, and offered to give him all the armour he needed.

Such was Erec's courage and resolve that he defeated his enemy with ease. He then married Enide and took her off to his own country where they began to share in a happiness that neither had ever dreamed possible. But such was Erec's love that he lost interest in all other things, even forsaking the acts of chivalry for which he was famed. He no longer went in search of adventure or even fought in tournaments. Most days, in fact, the couple did not leave their bed until noon. Erec's reputation was soon in tatters and people began to mock the once-proud knight behind his back, spreading rumours that he had become nothing more than a common coward.

The story of Erec and Enide was typical of many tales of courtly love in its emphasis on male derring-do and female virtue. The latter is evident in the well-known French tapestry *The Lady with the Unicorn*, replete with its rich floral and animal symbolism evoking beauty, purity, fidelity and courage.

The Gentle Art of Womanhood

Women were praised by poets and writers for many qualities, including their beauty, their manners and their faithfulness. In a world where male heroes were presented as paragons of action, however, perhaps the most extravagantly valued female attribute of all was docility.

As an example of incomparable virtue, Boccaccio, in his *Decameron,* told the tale of Griselda. She was a humble peasant who was chosen by Walter of Saluzzo to be his wife on the sole condition that she obey him without question.

Having agreed, she had to stand by while her children were taken from her, apparently to be put to death. Then, Walter told her he was to take a new wife, and she became the woman's servant. But Walter eventually revealed his demands were no more than tests of her love, and told Griselda that her tireless obedience had won his heart. At the end of the story, the children were brought back unharmed.

Petrarch thought the tale so uplifting that it should be told in Latin, and a French version filtered through to England, where Chaucer retold it in *The Canterbury Tales.* In all the versions, Griselda's behaviour was seen as exemplary and symbolic of the Virgin Mary.

Woman playing a viol, from *Des Cleres et Nobles Femmes*, Giovanni Boccaccio's treatise on the virtues of femininity, *c.*15th century.

Enide, however, was aware of the gossip and grew to hate it. One morning, she woke early and, thinking that Erec was asleep, gave vent to her sadness, bewailing aloud the shame she had brought upon him and wishing they had never even met. But Erec was only dozing, and when he heard what she was saying he leaped angrily from the bed and ordered her to dress. He then told her to mount a horse and ride ahead of him out of the castle and into the forest, threatening to punish her if she spoke to him without first being spoken to. He was going to take her on a long, dangerous journey so she could witness his courage.

With Enide riding on ahead, for all the world a solitary figure, it was not long before robbers and outlaw knights began to emerge from the forest's shadows eager for such vulnerable prey. Enide grew afraid, but whenever she turned to warn Erec he would condemn her for speaking out of turn. But then he would ride into view and attack the would-be assailants, killing them and stealing their horses. For all his threats, Enide kept on trying to save him from danger, and gradually Erec realized how much she loved him. He refused to end the quest, however, and with each fight he picked up more wounds and became a little weaker.

His greatest test came in a struggle with two giants who had kidnapped another knight. When Erec caught sight of them they had stripped the poor man naked, bound him to his horse and were striking him with great wooden clubs. Erec sprang into action, charging at one of the giants and stabbing him through the eye with his lance. But as he did so, the other struck Erec such a blow on his back that he was nearly knocked off his horse. Enraged, Erec turned sharply, drew his sword and with a single blow cleft the unfortunate giant in two.

He gave a great shout of triumph, but felt himself weakening from his injuries. Riding back to Enide he suddenly slipped from his saddle in a faint and crashed in a heap to the ground. Enide was seized with panic. Thinking he was dead, she began to wail, blaming herself for the tragedy and willing death to come for her too.

The sound of her sobs carried through the forest and was soon heard by a local count who was passing nearby with his attendants. Hurrying to the scene, he made a bier to transport Erec's body back to his palace. But from the moment he saw her, he too felt himself falling in love with the beautiful maiden who had wept so helplessly by her knight, and no sooner was Erec's broken body laid out on a dais in the main hall than the count began proposing marriage. Enide was shocked, and started crying inconsolably. The count grew angry, and in his fury at last hit her. There was a moment's silence, then uproar as the palace guests reacted to this terrible breach of the code of chivalry. The noise woke Erec who sprang up, grabbed his sword and charged at the shamed count, smashing his head with the hilt of his weapon and running him through with the blade. At once the attendants and knights all panicked and fled, terror-stricken at the sight of this vengeful corpse apparently returned to life.

Amid the confusion, Erec and Enide managed to escape from the palace. Back in the forest they were lucky to meet an honourable knight called Guivret the Little, who took Erec into his care and nursed his wounds until he was well.

Erec's last adventure took place on the journey home. While staying overnight in a town, he heard of a deadly challenge called "The Joy of the Court", which nobody had ever survived. Erec, flushed with so many recent victories, insisted on taking his chance, and was led to a garden where he saw a row of severed heads impaled on spikes. The last spike was empty, and Erec was told that it waited for him. There, watched by a beautiful woman on a silver couch, he defeated a gigantic knight called Mabonagrain, who, surprisingly, thanked him for the beating. It turned out that Mabonagrain was in love with the woman on the couch, and long ago had promised that he would remain with her in the garden forever, unless he was defeated in honest combat. By winning, Erec had set him free, and because Mabonagrain was the king's nephew, his release would lead to "The Joy of the Court". Then Enide had to console Mabonagrain's mistress that, being a gallant knight, the giant would continue to serve her even as a free man.

A knight's duty was to act faithfully on his mistress's wishes; her rejection for any reason provided only a further test of his devotion. This knight on horseback is actually a 13th-century copper aquamanile used to hold water for washing hands. The water entered through the helmet and was poured out through the horse's head.

Phantoms and Fantasies

While usually lauded as paragons of virtue, women were conversely sometimes seen as demons versed in the dark arts of seduction and sorcery. Witches and fays or fairies, meaning female beings with supernatural power, were feared for their ability to ensnare men as lovers. Their victims, however, were only too eager to be seduced.

Melusine was a water sprite who so fascinated people in the Middle Ages that several noble families, including Emperor Henry VII and the royal house of Luxembourg, claimed her as an ancestor.

According to a folklore tradition recorded by Jean d'Arras, she was one of three beautiful maidens who guarded a fountain deep in a forest. One day, the Count of Poitiers and his adopted son, Raymond, were tracking a boar in the woods when they became separated from their retinue. They stopped to make a fire when, suddenly, the boar burst from the bushes and ran straight at them. Raymond hewed at it with his sword but the blade bounced off the beast's thick hide and struck the count instead, killing him instantly. Raymond looked in horror at what he had done and, panicking, jumped on his horse and made off through the forest. Galloping blindly for some hours, he rode into a glade where he saw a bubbling fountain – and by its side three women so beautiful that Raymond thought they were angels.

One asked why he seemed so frightened, and when he told his story she advised him to return to Poitiers as if nothing had happened: since all the hunters had become separated, no one would know he had been with the count. Reassured by her words, he also felt himself drawn to her beauty. Raymond kept her talking until dawn, and before he left he begged her to be his wife. She agreed, telling him she was Melusine, a water sprite, and that near the fountain she would build them both a palace to be named Lusinia, after her. (A Lusignan Castle was built in Poitou by a powerful family of that name.) Her only condition was that he must never see her on a Saturday (the sabbath day for some), or they would be separated forever.

The couple lived happily together for some years, their only sadness being that all their children were disfigured in some way. The eldest son had drooping ears, and his eyes were of different colours, one red and one green. The second boy had a scarlet face, the third had one eye set higher than the other. The next child had claws on his fingers and hair all over his body, while a fifth son had just one eye. The sixth and youngest was given the name Geoffrey-with-the-Tooth because of a boar-like tusk in his lower jaw.

Despite these setbacks, however, the children grew up to be heroic and virtuous, and Raymond never stopped loving Melusine. Furthermore, he always respected her wish to be alone on Saturdays, suppressing his curiosity about the reason. But then, one day, one of his brothers told him that people in the town were gossiping. They were asking what unholy reason Melusine might have for never letting herself be seen on the sabbath.

Illustration to the story of Melusine, c.1401. This dutiful wife who was half-serpent, half-woman, was one of the most enduring of all French fictional characters and tales of her life spawned dozens of variants throughout Europe.

Hurrying to his wife's chambers, Raymond found them empty. When he discovered that the bathroom door was locked, he knelt to peer through the keyhole. What he saw shocked him: his wife was in the bath, but the lower half of her body had been transformed into a serpent's tail.

Because he still loved his wife, Raymond decided to keep his discovery secret. This he did, until one day news arrived that Geoffrey-with-the-Tooth had burned down the monastery of Malliers, killing the abbot and 100 monks, one of whom was an earlier child of Raymond's. When Melusine heard this, she rushed to comfort her husband, but in his grief he pushed her away, calling her an odious serpent who had contaminated his race.

Melusine fainted. When she recovered she began to cry before saying goodbye to her husband forever. She then ran to the window and flew off, leaving her two youngest children behind. Each night after that the nurses would see a ghostly figure with a serpent's tail appear by the children's side, suckling them like an attentive mother. By morning the spectre would be gone.

For hundreds of years afterwards it was said that Melusine would materialize on the ramparts of Lusignan whenever an old count was about to die, or a new one was due to be born. After the castle was destroyed in the sixteenth century, she was said to appear, wailing, to announce the death of the French king.

The Mysterious Swan Knight

Matching the tales featuring mysterious women were those with equally elusive male protagonists. One popular type was the swan knight story, of which there were many local variants. In these a heroic figure would appear, riding in a boat drawn by a swan, when summoned by a lady's prayer.

On his deathbed, the Duke of Brabant left his daughter Else in the care of a much-feared knight called Frederick, who wished to marry her. She refused, but Frederick got permission from the emperor to win her by right of combat, against any champion she chose.

Hard as she tried, she could not find anyone prepared to fight Frederick. However, her predicament started a magic bell ringing in the blessed land of the Holy Grail, the cup used to offer the first communion at the Last Supper. The sound of the bell summoned Lohengrin, the son of the Grail's guardian, to aid her.

Lohengrin was about to mount his horse and set off when he saw a swan on the river, pulling a shallow boat, and he realized that it had come for him.

In Brabant, the day for the contest arrived, and, without a challenger, Frederick was about to claim Else. Whereupon the swan-drawn boat drew up to the riverbank, with Lohengrin inside, sleeping on his shield. Waking, he leaped onto the shore, and the swan swam off.

Lohengrin then fought and killed Frederick, and Else offered herself and her lands to him. He accepted, but only on condition that she never ask him where he came from.

They lived happily for several years, but after Lohengrin broke a knight's arm in a tournament, the man's wife began to question his past. When Else heard this, she cried every night until at last she asked Lohengrin where he was from. He told her, but at dawn the next day the swan came for him and he departed.

Similar stories included one about Helias, who married the Duchess of Cleves then left when she asked him about his origins, and another about a mute knight found by Charlemagne drifting up the Rhine in a swan-borne boat with a sign on him declaring that he had come in search of a wife and lands. As the legend spread, the stranger was said to have been an ancestor of the crusader Godfrey de Bouillon.

The Curse of the Sabbath

A variant of the Melusine story told how Fulke, Count of Angiers, married a beautiful woman and had four healthy children. He became concerned, however, by the fact that his wife always left church before Communion. So one day Fulke had four of his knights stand on her cloak to see how she would react. Just before the consecration of the Host, she claimed to have forgotten something but as she rose to leave she found herself trapped. She began to panic, and as the Host was raised, she screamed and fled from the church, carrying two of her children with her. The two children who remained were the ancestors of the counts of Anjou, including Raymond of Poitiers.

Jean d'Arras wrote that Melusine was born from the union of Helmas, a king of Scotland, and a fairy called Pressina who he had met by a fountain. She agreed to marry the king so long as he swore never to visit her as she lay in bed in the morning. When, soon afterwards, Helmas heard that his wife had given birth to three daughters – Melusine, Melior and Plantina – he hurried to her side. But as he entered the room, an angry Pressina snatched up her children and fled.

Fifteen years later, Pressina told her daughters what had happened all those years previously. Hearing that her father had broken the promise he had made to her mother, Melusine decided to punish him further by having him chained up inside a mountain. But when Pressina heard what her daughter had done, she cursed her to spend every future sabbath only half human. The curse would only be broken if she could find a husband who would never ask why she refused to be seen on that day.

Melior and Partonope

A similar story featured Melusine's sister, Melior. This romance, dating from about 1188, told how Partonope of Blois, the nephew of a French king, was out hunting boar when he stumbled on an enchanted boat which carried him to a strange castle. There he was fed by invisible servants and taken to bed by an unseen fairy princess called Melior. She said she would marry him so long as he never tried to look on her.

A year later Partonope had to hurry home to help defend his country from Danish invaders. He was hailed as a hero, but soon after winning a great victory he was tricked by his sorceress mother into proposing to a niece of the king. He soon recovered his senses, however, and, rejecting this new wife at once, announced his intention to return to his true love.

His scheming mother then gave Partonope a magic lantern. On his first night back with Melior, a beam of light caught her, and Partonope saw that she was the most beautiful woman who had ever been born. But she fainted, and upon her recovery she told him that his betrayal had cost her all her powers. She sent him home, where he wandered despairingly until he met Melior's sister, here called Urrake, in a forest. She restored him to sanity, and explained that a three-day tournament was to be held with Melior's hand as the prize. And with Urrake's help, Partonope won the tournament and regained the love of Melior.

A gold ciborium, used to cover the Host during Mass, made in Limoges for Montmajour Abbey, 13th century. Women who left church suspiciously before Communion were a common subject of medieval folklore.

73

The Rages of Jealousy

Although adulterous passion was extolled in courtly poems, it was generally idealized and unrequited. In the real world, marital infidelity was a cause of scandal and revenge, and a number of legends and ballads recognized this in their depictions of female malevolence.

Henry II, king of England, had several mistresses. The most famous of them was Rosamond, daughter of a minor nobleman called Walter de Clifford. She became the subject of a popular ballad that simultaneously celebrated her beauty, mourned her death and slandered the king's wife, Eleanor of Aquitaine.

According to the ballad, Rosamond was so lovely that she was known as "the rose of the world". Henry, deeply jealous of any man who even so much as looked at her, built a labyrinthine house for her on the royal estate at Woodstock. The design was so cunning that nobody could find a way through without the aid of a length of thread to mark the proper path.

In 1173, Henry had to go to France to put down a revolt, instigated in part by his wife and led by his own sons. Rosamond begged him to take her with him, but he refused, saying that she would be safer in England, and that he would entrust a knight to guard her. But as soon as he left the country, Henry's jealous wife, Eleanor, went to Woodstock with a company of men. They called to the knight, and when he emerged, holding one

end of the thread, they killed him and followed it back to Rosamond. When Eleanor saw for herself how lovely this woman really was, it only made her more angry. She ordered her rival to shed her silk gowns and prepare to die as she chose: by sword or poison.

Rosamond fell to her knees and begged for her life. She promised to enter a convent if she were spared, but although she was crying and wiping her eyes, her beauty remained unstained, enraging the jealous queen still further. Eventually, resigned to her fate, Rosamond rose to drink the poison. She emptied the cup that Eleanor had prepared for her and moments later lay lifeless upon the floor. But Eleanor took little pleasure in her revenge. She saw that, even in death, Rosamond remained the rose of the world.

While it is true that Henry had a house built for Rosamond on the royal estate, it is likely that the "labyrinth" of the tale was no more than an adjoining garden maze. Rosamond was not killed by Eleanor of Aquitaine, but entered Godstow Nunnery of her own volition. Even in her own lifetime, however, Eleanor was already being described as a she-demon at whose door all kinds of vices and misdeeds were laid.

The Ballad of Clerk Covill

This was not only true of Eleanor. In general, medieval folk histories tended to portray women's sexual jealousy as some kind of insatiable, demonic force that would crush the very petals of the flowers which honourable knights would have had them cherish. By the same token, malevolent female sprites were said to covet Christian men on the eve of their wedding.

A margin illumination from the 14th-century *Luttrell Psalter* shows a wife beating her husband with a distaff. Such realistic vignettes suggest that medieval women were in fact far from always being the docile spirits pictured in the romances.

An eerie Scottish ballad begins with Clerk Covill's betrothed warning him that, for the sake of their future together, he should never ride near a mysterious place known as the wells of Slane. But, his curiosity aroused, he ignored her and set off for that very spot. When he reached the water's edge he saw a woman washing herself and her clothing. He called out to her not to stop on his account, and she answered flirtatiously that she was glad to see a man there with such fine, milky skin. But Covill suddenly felt his head begin to ache, and he grew pale as his strength slipped slowly away. When he complained of his ailment, the woman invited him to cut a bandage from her gown. She bound the fabric round his head herself, but Covill found the pain only got worse. When he told her, she replied that it would grow increasingly more acute until it killed him. As Covill drew his sword to slay her, she turned into a fish and swam away.

Eleanor of Aquitaine, Powerful Patroness

Wife of two kings and mother of two more, Eleanor was the most influential women of her time. A power-broker and patroness of the arts, her life was obscured from an early age by legend.

Eleanor was born in 1122, the granddaughter of William IX, the Duke of Aquitaine and Count of Poitiers. At the age of twenty-five she accompanied her husband, King Louis VII of France, on the Second Crusade, and scurrilous rumours were soon spreading about her behaviour in the Holy Land. Some said that she had had an affair in Antioch with her uncle, Prince Raymond. Others claimed that she had fallen in love with Saladin himself and sent an interpreter to the Saracen leader bearing an invitation for him to abduct her.

Whatever really happened, she and Louis divorced, officially on the grounds that she had failed to produce a male heir. Six months later, in 1152, she married Henry of Anjou who became Henry II of England.

Her unpredictable nature, however, was not tamed. She bore Henry eight children and when her sons were grown up she encouraged them to rebel against their father. Henry had her imprisoned for ten years, but after his death she began to exert a powerful influence over his heirs, Richard and John.

During her time in prison, further rumours began to spread. It was said that as queen of France, she had enjoyed an adulterous affair with Geoffrey, Count of Anjou and the father of her husband, Henry. What was more, the rumours went, Henry knew this, for as a youth he had stood guard at their trysts. Later writers, such as Gerald of Wales, claimed that this behaviour had cursed the family, and caused the quarrels that plagued it.

The tomb of Eleanor of Aquitaine, at Fontevrault Abbey, near Tours.

The Lais *of Marie de France*

From skilfully adulterous wives to resourceful young lovers, some of the liveliest and most independently minded women in medieval folklore are found in the short poems of the female author known today simply as Marie de France.

The real identity of the twelfth-century poet known as Marie de France remains the subject of a fierce historical debate – contenders range from Marie de Champagne, the daughter of Eleanor of Aquitaine and a great patroness of the arts, to Marie the Abbess of Shaftesbury, who was half-sister to Henry II, and Marie the Countess of Boulogne, who was an abbess in Hampshire before being married off to further the king's political ends. But while her profile as a historical figure has faded over time, Marie de France's stories have lost none of the clarity and power they had when they were first recounted to the Plantagenet court of England.

Marie wrote in vernacular French, and took as her form the lays or *lais* – narrative songs that had become the stock-in-trade of the poets of Brittany. Her poems retain the brevity of ballads while displaying particular insights that could only, perhaps, have come from a woman. For example, Marie shows a powerful sympathy for those women who had been forced into tyrannical marriages with older men – most evidently in what was perhaps her first *lai*, where she describes a handsome young nobleman called Guigemar who claimed he was incapable of falling in love, despite being pursued by every lady in Britanny.

The Lovers' Vow

One day, when Guigemar was out hunting he spotted a deer with magnificent antlers. With a single movement he raised his bow and loosed an arrow that struck the animal on the head. The deer was felled instantly but the arrow rebounded and caught Guigemar painfully in the thigh. The mortally wounded creature then spoke to Guigemar, cursing him that his thigh would never heal until it was tended by a woman who would suffer terribly for his love, and who would make him suffer similarly. Delirious with agony and fear, Guigemar hurried to escape from the forest and soon found himself at a strange harbour, where a magical boat awaited him.

He struggled aboard but found the vessel crewless. Then, noticing a sumptuous, golden bed, he lay down on it and fell asleep immediately. The boat carried him to an ancient city, ruled by a jealous old man who had imprisoned his wife in an impenetrable enclosure. On three sides it was surrounded by high walls and on the fourth by the sea. Inside she was attended by a maid and guarded by a eunuch. When she saw the boat approaching her prison, she waited for it to dock, then went on board. Finding Guigemar, she decided to hide him in her quarters.

There, in secret, Guigemar stayed and soon enough he fell in love with his keeper. Shortly the agony of not being able to tell her what he felt was greater than the pain of his wound. The maid, however, spotted that her mistress was also in love and, acting as a go-between, she succeeded in manoeuvring them together until, finally, they consummated their passion.

Over time, Guigemar recovered. He spent some eighteen months in the lady's chambers until, one fateful day, the couple were discovered. Realizing that they were about to be separated, and fearful that he would find another consort, the woman tied a knot in his shirt and made him vow not to love anyone who could not untie it. He then knotted a belt around her hips, and extracted the same promise from her. Then he boarded the magic boat and sailed back to his own land.

A Fairer View of Womanhood

*The first woman known to have supported herself entirely by writing, Christine de Pisan applied her wits eclectically: poems of courtly love, **lais**, even a biography of Charles V. And she also produced many "complaints", championing the cause of medieval women.*

Christine was the daughter of a court astrologer to the French king, Charles V. She began to write in 1389, at the age of twenty-five, after her husband of ten years died and left her to bring up their three children. Her first poems were love ballads addressed to her dead husband, which proved so popular that she was able to take up writing full time. Her fame spread quickly.

Christine was always vociferous in her praise of women. Her *Letter to the God of Love*, written in 1399, was an answer to the woman-baiting attitudes of Jean de Meun, who completed the popular *Roman de la Rose*. Although the *Roman* was begun by Guillaume de Lorris as an allegory, modelled on Ovid's *Art of Love*, about wooing a maiden symbolized as a rosebud, in de Meun's hands it became a huge, quarrelsome – and occasionally misogynistic – epic.

Christine also wrote *The Book of the City of Ladies*, a collection of lives of women who were known for their heroism and virtues, while her last work was an ecstatic celebration of the early victories of Joan of Arc.

Christine de Pisan writing at her desk, from a 15th-century manuscript. As one of the few woman writers of prose romance, Christine was able to render female characters more accurately than many of her male colleagues.

Guigemar insisted on knotting his lover's belt himself to ensure her chastity. Gold buckle, from northern Lombardy.

There, his people wanted him to marry, but none of the contenders for his hand could undo the knot. His lost lover, meanwhile was shut in a tower, fighting the madness of solitude. When, one day, she discovered her room unlocked, she ran to the sea to drown herself. But there she saw the magic boat and immediately climbed on board.

The boat carried her to a Breton realm ruled by a king called Meriaduc. He fell in love with her but since he could not untie her belt, she refused his advances. He was furious and at his next tournament brought the lady forward as a game to amuse the assembled knights. Among them was Guigemar, who stepped forward and undid the belt. Meriaduc refused to give her up, so Guigemar drew his sword and slew him. Then he took his lady by the hand and led her happily away.

The Power of Love

The lover's vow appears again in Marie's story of the impoverished knight Lanval. When resting in a meadow one day, Lanval met two fairy maidens who took him to their mistress. Wanting him as her lover, she made a declaration that had one condition. She would appear to him any time he wished and make him rich beyond his dreams. But he must always be alone, for if he ever told anyone about her, she would abandon him forever.

Lanval was delighted and very soon was living a happy life of wealth. Then, one day, Queen Guinevere tried to seduce him. When he rejected her, she accused him of not liking women. He replied that he not only had a lover but one who made Guinevere look plain. And then, to his horror, he realized he had broken his word.

Matters got worse, however, for the queen accused him of trying to seduce her and Lanval found himself on trial before the king. After hearing his defence, the court decided that if he could produce a lady who did indeed outshine the queen, he would go free; if not, he would die. The sorry knight was reconciled to death, but at the last moment his mistress appeared before the judges to explain that, although he had betrayed her, she did not want him to come to any harm. Even the king agreed that she was lovelier than the queen, and Lanval was freed.

If Marie favoured loyalty, she also deplored excess or vanity. A *lai* called *Les Deux Amanz*, told of a king who doted on his daughter so much that he would let no man marry her who could not carry her to the top of a nearby mountain. Many tried, but none succeeded. All this time, the princess was in love with a young man who had been persuading her to elope. She was unwilling to betray her father, so came up with another plan.

She told her admirer to visit a relative of hers who could prepare a potion to give him the strength to carry her to the top of the mountain. While he was away, the princess fasted to make his task easier, and on his return, she wore as little clothing as was decent. Giving her the phial to hold, he began to carry her up the steep slope. Half-way up, she urged him to swallow the potion, but having brought her so far without any help, his vanity got the better of him and he refused. As he reached the summit, however, his heart gave out and he fell dead, and the girl then died from grief beside him. The *lai* ends with the couple being laid to rest in a marble coffin and buried on the mountain-top by the mourning king.

The Knight and the Shadow

Another thirteenth-century writer of *lais*, Jean Renart, only ever signed his name to one poem, the *Lai de L'Ombre*. In the twentieth century, anagrams of his name were discovered in two other manuscripts, a verse adventure called *L'Escoufle* – about two betrothed children who elope when the emperor tries to separate them – and a romance called *Guillaume de Dole*, about a woman's efforts to defend her name after being accused of adultery. Both are now accepted as his work.

The *Lai de L'Ombre*, though, remains Renart's masterpiece. Completed between 1217 and 1221, it tells the story of a knight who came to visit the most well-bred lady in the land. Finding her sitting in a garden by a well, he approached to offer her his love with the gift of a ring. When she refused him, he asked if he could at least have one of her gloves as a token. She agreed, but as she removed it from her hand, he slipped his ring onto her finger. The lady insisted that he remove it at once and despite his most eloquent arguments, he could find no way of persuading her to keep it. Eventually he took the band from her and placed it on the shadow of her hand in the well. When she asked what he was doing, he explained that since she would not love him, he would have the love of the shadow instead, and that even this would be better than any other woman. The lady was so charmed by the gesture that she finally agreed to be his.

The Pyrenees range in southwest France. Marie de France's story *Les Deux Amanz* describes how a knight is challenged to carry his love to the top of a mountain. Rejecting the magical help she offers he dies of exhaustion when they get there.

The Fairy Kingdoms

It was widely thought that fairies, or fays, were insatiably curious, with a love of novelty and beauty, but that they had no independent powers of procreation. And that was why it was believed they liked to abduct humans to be their companions, lovers or offspring.

A number of classical myths made their way into the songs and romances of the Middle Ages, often via the poetry of Ovid or Virgil. Both of these influential authors wrote versions of one of the oldest Greek myths of all, *Orpheus and Eurydice*. Orpheus was a Thracian master musician who followed his dead wife into the underworld and persuaded its king to release her. Hades's ruler set one condition: that Orpheus would not turn to look at her until they reached the surface. Tragically, he failed to keep his promise and lost her forever.

The Story of Orfeo and Heurodis

Medieval poets replaced the classical underworld of Hades with a fairy kingdom otherworld of their own invention, and, most crucially, gave the tale a happy ending. A French *Lai d'Orphy*, dating back to the twelfth century, seems to have existed at one time, but the best known surviving medieval adaptation of the myth is *Sir Orfeo*, written by an anonymous Englishman not long before 1330.

The author states that the city of Winchester used to be called Thrace, and that its king, Sir Orfeo, was the finest harpist in the land. One May morning his wife, Heurodis, was sleeping under a tree in the orchard when she suddenly sat bolt upright and began to thrash and scream, clawing at her face with her nails. She later explained that she had seen a vision of a mysterious king, wearing a crown heavy with gemstones and accompanied by 100 knights and 100 ladies. This magnificent monarch had then proceeded to tell her that he would return the next day and take her off to live with him forever, even if he had to rip her limb from limb in the process.

Orfeo at once deployed 1,000 knights to guard his queen but even though they kept her completely surrounded by night and day, she still disappeared. When he heard the news, Orfeo was heartbroken and he vowed that he would leave his kingdom to live in the wilderness, where he would never set eyes on another woman again. He handed power over to his steward, donned a rough pilgrim's gown and departed the castle barefoot carrying nothing save for his harp.

For ten long years he lived by digging for roots and picking berries, sleeping on the bare ground with only leaves and twigs for a blanket. He kept his harp safe in a hollowed tree, and when he played it all the birds and animals of the forest would

The realm that Orfeo found in the forest was one where jewels dazzled in magical abundance. To the average peasant of the Middle Ages, this 13th-century crown would have seemed an appropriate item for any fairy king.

gather round to listen. Although he shunned the company of people, sometimes he would see knights and their ladies riding past in the woods. Occasionally, he thought he even glimpsed the fairy king himself, riding out on a hunt.

Then, one day, he saw an unaccompanied group of women, using hawks to hunt for wild-fowl. The birds of prey fascinated Orfeo, and he watched them climb high into the air and then swoop swiftly to the ground. Suddenly, he saw Heurodis among the company. Although Orfeo was dressed in rags and had a waist-length black beard, she also recognized him. They were too shocked to speak, and stared dumbly at each other with tears pouring down their cheeks. But when Heurodis's companions saw this, they hustled her quickly away.

Orfeo decided to follow them wherever they went. Eventually he tracked them to a cleft in some rocks. He crept carefully inside and found himself in the fairy realm standing before the jew-elled walls of a vast castle, its towers shining as brightly as the sun. Orfeo walked nervously up to

Set among medieval society's better-off classes, many Middle Ages' romances featured women being wooed within the safety of their family castles or in formal court settings – for as the tale of Lady Isabel suggested, many dangers lurked beyond the walls of "civilization". Gardens, in this context, provided an in-between, cultivated natural setting for private courtship to take place, as seen in the *Garden of Love* by Loyset Liedet, *c.1470*.

the gates and, after claiming to be a wandering minstrel, was welcomed inside. There he saw great rows of statues which he soon realized were the bodies of people who had been stolen by the fairies, frozen exactly as they had been when they were taken. He began looking frantically for his wife. After ascertaining that she was indeed there, he approached the king and asked if he might play his harp for the court.

The king – not recognizing Orfeo and think-ing him a fool to have entered fairyland of his own free will – gave his permission, and from the first sweet notes that dropped from Orfeo's harp the whole court was enchanted by his playing. When the music eventually finished, the now-tearful king

81

offered its creator anything he cared to ask for as payment. Orfeo did not need to pause for thought. He immediately declared his desire for the beautiful woman he had seen sleeping in the courtyard.

At this request the king's mood changed utterly. He raged in anger, appalled at the thought of giving his beautiful mistress to such an unkempt vagabond. Orfeo, however, persisted, reminding the fairy king that he had made an offer, and that a king should keep his promise.

The fairy king shook with fury, but at last he relented. Orfeo took his wife by the hand and led her back to Winchester. Hiding her in a beggar's house, he then went to the castle and offered to play for his steward. The old adviser immediately recognized the harp as belonging to Orfeo. Puzzled, he asked where it had come from. To test his loyalty, Orfeo pretended that he had taken it from a man's corpse, eaten by wolves. When the steward began to cry for his dead master, Orfeo revealed himself as the king, praised the steward and ordered him to send for the queen. And with everything once more in place, he at last resumed his throne, his beloved wife back at his side.

A Marriage Pact and a Lost Kingdom

Crucial to a number of "fairy" stories were the beliefs that in the otherworld time ran at a different rate, and, because not everything was always as it seemed, that it was dangerous to accept magic gifts. A number of stories concern one or the other topics, but the tale of Herla combines both.

Herla was a British king who, while out hunting, met a red-bearded dwarf riding a goat. The dwarf told Herla that he would soon be visited by ambassadors offering the hand of a French princess in marriage. The stranger promised to attend the wedding feast and insisted that Herla return the compliment a year later. When the king returned to his castle, the ambassadors were already there.

On the day of the nuptials, the dwarf arrived with a multitude of courtiers and servants, who provided food and drink for all the guests before magically vanishing at the first cock's crow. Exactly a year on, the dwarf appeared again to remind Herla that it was time to repay his debt. The king called his retinue, telling them to bring as much food and wine as they could carry, and followed the dwarf on a journey into wild countryside. They entered a deep cavern, leading to a brightly lit hall, where they celebrated the dwarf's marriage.

The next day Herla and his men mounted their horses and left, loaded down with gifts, including a small bloodhound which was carried by the king. The dwarf told Herla that nobody could dismount until the hound had leaped from his arms. When they left the cavern they met an old man, introduced themselves and asked for news. But he told them he could barely understand them; he was a Saxon and they were speaking a Celtic tongue. King Herla, he said, had disappeared hundreds of years ago. When two of Herla's courtiers climbed down to interrogate him, they turned to dust. The story ends by saying that since the dog has not yet left Herla's arms, he and his men are condemned to wander forever.

A Lie in the House of Love

Sometimes mortal danger also lay in apparent romance. In ballads, most kidnapped heroines had to be rescued by their knights or husbands, but some were more independently resourceful. A Scottish ballad began on the first morning in May with Lady Isabel, a princess, sitting in her room sewing. She heard an elf-knight blowing his hunting horn and idly wished that he would come to visit her and lay his head on her breast. No sooner had she spoken than he appeared at her window, insisting that she follow him into the woods.

She went willingly, but when they stopped he told her that he had killed seven princesses on the very spot, and that she was to be the eighth. Isabel asked him to wait a while and rest his head on her knee. She stroked his hair until he began to doze, whereupon she took his own sword and stabbed him to death. As she left, she drew the moral: "If you have slain seven king's daughters here, then lie here as husband to them."

True Thomas of Erceldoune

Thomas the Rhymer, or True Thomas as he is also known, was a famous character from Scottish folklore. It was said that an elf-queen granted him the gift of always telling the truth.

Thomas was resting on the banks of a ravine when he saw a woman riding towards him. She was so lovely that, when she came near, he asked if she were the queen of heaven. "No," she answered, "I am the queen of elfland." She then explained that she had come to take Thomas to live with her for seven years, and that if he kissed her he would be under her spell.

Thomas promptly climbed on to the back of her horse. The pair flew like the wind until they came to a fragrant garden. Thomas wanted to eat some of its fruit, but the elf-queen warned him that it contained the plagues of all humankind. She gave him bread and wine, and after he had eaten she pointed out the three paths that led from the garden.

The first one, winding through prickly briers, was the path of righteousness. The second, running through a lily field, was the way of wickedness. The third led to elfland – but before they took it the queen warned Thomas not to say a word while in her country, or he would not get back to his own land.

They travelled for forty days and nights, and encountered rivers of blood; thus filled, explained the queen, because all the blood spilled in the world ran through the springs of elfland.

At last they reached her garden, and she gave Thomas an apple which, once eaten, would prevent him from ever telling a lie when he went back to his own land.

Thomas ended up staying in elfland for seven years and when he finally returned home, he won a reputation as a great prophet, for all the predictions he made about the future turned out to be true.

Loves Lost and Found

In many romances, love was seen as the supreme duty of a knight, and the search for it meant overcoming tremendous obstacles on the way. There was no greater impediment to a happy unison, however, than the clash of faiths, and thus the theme of a forbidden amour between Christian and pagan became a favourite one for medieval authors and translators.

The story of Floire and Blancheflor was one of Giovanni Boccaccio's most famous tales, but variants of the same plotline can be found in old French, English and Spanish versions. There is even an Icelandic account, based on a long-lost Norse translation.

The story concerns a pregnant countess who, after becoming widowed, set off with her father on a pilgrimage to give thanks for her unborn child. On the journey the pair were attacked by a Saracen king called Felix, whose soldiers killed the old man and took the countess prisoner.

Felix's wife was also pregnant, and the two women soon became friends. By a miracle, they both gave birth on Palm Sunday, the queen to a boy called Floire, and the countess to a girl named Blancheflor. As they grew up together, the children became inseparable and fell in love. But

A 12th-century chess piece from the Isle of Lewis, Scotland. The cunning Floire gained entry to the tower where his beloved Blancheflor was held by beating the porter at a game of chess the gullible man was convinced he would win.

Felix would not tolerate his son's affection for a Christian, and with his wife he plotted to separate the young couple. The king sold Blancheflor to slave-traders, but to hide what he had done he ordered the construction of a richly decorated mausoleum, and told Floire that his beloved had died and been entombed there.

Floire was so distraught that he stopped eating. Realizing that he might die of grief, the queen confessed that Blancheflor was still alive, held captive in Cairo as part of the emir's harem.

Floire immediately set off to rescue her. In Cairo, he discovered that Blancheflor was held in a keep with all the rest of the emir's maidens and he set off to investigate. The tower turned out to be surrounded by an exotic garden at the centre of which stood a magic tree. Each day, as the girls exercised, the tree would drop a single flower on one of them. The unlucky girl was then taken to the emir's bed for the night, and was beheaded the next morning. Floire, realizing that it could soon be the turn of his beloved Blancheflor to be called to this wretched fate, set about finding a way into the tower.

After observing the building for some hours, Floire noticed that the tower's porter spent much of the time gambling. So, picking his moment carefully, he wandered over and challenged the man to a game of chess. Floire let the porter win the first games. When he was giddy at the sight of his winnings, Floire increased the stakes: if he lost the next game, he would have to smuggle his challenger inside the tower. Floire had no difficulty winning the crucial match and, as agreed, was carried into the tower hidden in a basket of flowers.

The next day, while the rest of the harem girls were walking in the garden, the reunited lovers lay in each others' arms. But the emir had been watching the women closely and he noticed one was absent. Growing suspicious, he ran up to the harem quarters where he discovered Floire and

Blancheflor alone together. The ruler flew into a jealous rage and condemned them both to be burned at the stake.

Now before Floire had left home, his mother had given him a magical ring which protected its wearer from any harm. So as the lovers stood awaiting the flames, Floire put the ring on Blancheflor's finger. But she refused to take it and handed it back, insisting that he wear it instead. Again he forced it onto her finger, only for her to return it once more. Their argument continued, and they grew angrier and angrier, raising their voices as each insisted that the other should be saved – until, at last, Blancheflor threw the ring to the floor in recognition that their fates were hopelessly entwined. And there, together, they awaited the flames. The emir, however, had overheard their angry exchanges and was so impressed with the selflessness of their love that he decided to release them at once. They left Cairo as soon as they could and travelled to Spain, where Floire was converted to Christianity and the two were married.

Aucassin and Nicolette

Another story with a similar theme concerned Nicolette, the pagan daughter of the king of Carthage. When she was a child she was stolen by slave-traders and ended up in the service of the captain of a city called Beaucaire (near Arles in modern Provence) who raised her as a Christian. One day, she came to the attention of the son of the Count of Beaucaire, the brave and noble

French 16th-century tapestry entitled _La Vie Seigneuriale_. For medieval artists gardens represented the ideals of order and harmony. For Blancheflor, however, the garden of the emir threatened an imminent death.

Aucassin, who was captivated by her beauty. The young man learned her name, and henceforth her charm and grace occupied his thoughts entirely. He forsook the arts of war in which he had excelled and took to daydreaming about the exotic slave-girl he had seen that day.

So love-struck did he become that when, shortly afterwards, the city came under siege, Aucassin refused to fight. His father pleaded with him, but the son simply replied that he was in love with Nicolette and could think of nothing else. Outraged, the count immediately ordered his

A friend then persuaded a pining Aucassin to go for a ride in the woods, hoping that it might ease his mind. On the forest path the knight met a shepherd who told him that an impossibly beautiful woman had passed that way the day before. Aucassin was suddenly filled with hope and set off desperately into the forest depths. And there he found her, running as hard as she could towards him. Laughing with delight, she told him that the captain had locked her in a tower from which she escaped using her sheets as a rope.

They ran away together, but their happiness was short-lived. They fetched up in a land called Torelore, topsy-turvy world where the king suffered labour pains while his queen led the army, and where the soldiers used food for weapons. When the country was invaded by Saracens the two lovers were separated again.

Aucassin returned to Beaucaire, where he learned that his father was dead, while Nicolette was taken back to Carthage. There she was reunited with her father, but when he tried to marry her off to one of his allies she refused. Instead she learned to play the viola before setting off once more, her face darkened with berries, to make her way as a minstrel until she found Aucassin again. Once back in Beaucaire, she went straight to the castle to sing about the adventures of a lady called Nicolette. Aucassin, moved to tears, offered the singer a fortune to bring his beloved back from Carthage. Seeing that his passion was undimmed, she promised she could do even better and show him that which he loved most – and with that she washed her brown-stained face clean before his disbelieving eyes to reveal her true identity.

captain to send the troublesome girl overseas – otherwise, he said, he would have her burned at the stake. When Aucassin found out, he offered to fight the invaders – but only if he could see Nicolette one final time. His father agreed, but as soon as Aucassin had led his countrymen to victory and taken the enemy leader captive, the count declared that his beloved had already been taken abroad and could no longer be found. Aucassin was furious. He released his prisoner, but not before he made the man vow to do as much harm to the count as he possibly could.

Medieval images of lovers, like the one shown on this plate from Italy, often emphasized calm and tranquillity, although many of the romances took the opposite tack.

The Worth of Hynd Horn

While there were medieval stories about love across class boundaries, most romance occurred between social equals. Even when one of the lovers appeared to be a slave or peasant, a twist in the tale usually revealed that they were nobly born. Birth-status notwithstanding, in a number of tales a knight would go on a quest in pursuit of glory so that he might deserve his beloved when he returned.

Although he was of noble birth, Hynd Horn was not rich and worked as a servant at the court of the king. One day he was spotted by the king's daughter, who immediately fell in love with him. She begged him to marry her, but he protested that he was not wealthy enough to marry a princess, and would only agree if her father knighted him first.

The girl persuaded her father, and as soon as Hynd was a knight, she began to pester him again to marry her. This time, though, he insisted that he must first prove himself in combat before he could be deemed worthy of her.

Before he departed, the princess gave him a special ring. If it ever lost its gleam, she warned, he would have lost her to another man.

For seven years he travelled in foreign countries, often looking at the ring, until, at last, one day he noticed that it had become tarnished.

Returning home swiftly, he met a beggar, who told him that the princess had been married for nine days, but she was refusing to go to her husband's bed until she heard news of Hynd Horn. Hearing this, Hynd swapped his clothes for the rags belonging to the beggar and went promptly to the palace where the couple lived.

At the gate, he asked for a drink served by the bride's own hand. The princess brought him a goblet, and after draining it he slipped the ring inside. She asked who had given him the ring, and he replied that she had, long ago. At that, the princess recognized him, and left her husband to ran away with Hynd Horn.

THE FLOWERING OF LOVE

One of the most enduring images of medieval life is the gallant knight offering himself to the service of a fair maiden. The chivalric code which this vision encapsulates grew not from the actual deeds of knights themselves, however, but from the lyrical songs of Languedoc troubadours. These minstrels spawned a literary tradition which spread throughout twelfth-century Europe and culminated in the French *Roman de la Rose*, perhaps the finest literary expression of the genre. The work presented its heroine as a rose kept safe inside the garden of courtly society. It was a gentle allegory that mixed spiritual and contemplative themes with bawdy and satirical ones. And by reflecting a broad cross-section of medieval life, the poem showed that its authors were alive to the irony that their rich and gentle poetic tradition grew from a very different reality.

Above: The literature of the later Middle Ages drew on the songs of wandering minstrels. Detail from an illustration to *The Book of Songs*; Spanish, 13th century.

Left: A woman's unattainability was a crucial part of the chivalric code, which insisted that a knight suffer heroically to earn his mistress's love. A woman who gave in too easily to his overtures was scorned as being morally wanting. This picture of a warrior rescuing a maiden in a particularly daring feat of bravery is from an illustration to Christine de Pisan's *Epitre d'Othea, c.*15th century.

Below: Florentine marriage chest decorated with scenes of courtly love, *c.*1350. Idealized visions of faithful love were not the only staple of medieval stories, however. Many tales told of adulterous exploits and subterfuge in which a chest might be used to smuggle an illicit lover into a bedchamber.

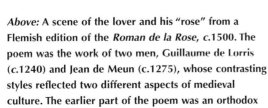

Above: A scene of the lover and his "rose" from a Flemish edition of the *Roman de la Rose, c.*1500. The poem was the work of two men, Guillaume de Lorris (*c.*1240) and Jean de Meun (c.1275), whose contrasting styles reflected two different aspects of medieval culture. The earlier part of the poem was an orthodox parable of idealized love. De Meun's contribution was very different, its many philosophical, scientific and often bawdy digressions helping to ensure the poem's enduring appeal. The work influenced other pieces as varied as Dante's *La Vita Nuova*, and Geoffrey Chaucer's *Troilus and Criseyde*.

OUTLAWS AND CHAMPIONS OF JUSTICE

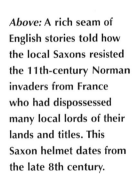

Alongside the romances, another, more realistic story-telling tradition developed in the course of the Middle Ages. To start with at least, it shared many of the conventions of the courtly sagas, for the audience was often the same. But over the centuries, the genre, which described the fight of individuals outside the law against injustice or oppression, developed a life of its own. Its heroes increasingly came from real places and fought against recognizable social wrongs.

The tradition first developed in England, where it grew out of popular tales of the struggle of the Saxon natives against foreign incursion around the time of the Norman Conquest. Hereward and Edric, for example, were both members of the old land-owning class who were dispossessed by the country's Norman invaders. Even Guy of Warwick, in many ways a conventional courtly knight of the old school, was linked to the new breed of hero by his fight against the Danes whose raids had devastated much of England in the preceding centuries.

Yet, curiously, the stories proved almost as popular across the Channel. Like Hereward, Eustace the Monk, from the Boulogne region of Normandy, saw his father's lands unjustly appropriated and took up arms to seek redress. Robert le Diable was a Norman aristocrat whose diabolical origins forced him beyond the law. And by the late Middle Ages the vogue had reached Switzerland and taken on a political edge, providing a focal hero for the struggle for independence from Austria in the figure of William Tell.

A common feature of most of the stories was the hero's flight into the wilderness, where the law's writ did not run. For Hereward this meant the Cambridgeshire fens and for Eustace the high seas; but more usually it involved taking to the forest, the natural base of the most enduring of all outlaw heroes, Robin Hood. At once familiar and yet remote, the greenwood was a subject of endless fascination to those who lived among the tamed, open fields. Dark and threatening, it haunted their imagination as a place in whose remote fastnesses fantastic adventure might lurk – an alternative world of mystery, all the more compelling as it lay so close to home.

Above: **A rich seam of English stories told how the local Saxons resisted the 11th-century Norman invaders from France who had dispossessed many local lords of their lands and titles. This Saxon helmet dates from the late 8th century.**

Opposite: **The British countryside was once dominated by woodland, an ideal refuge for outlaws and, to the medieval mind, a place of great imaginary power where danger and mystery lurked omnipresent in the dark, leafy shadows.**

91

The Fighter in the Fens

Saxon England's greatest hero fought a doomed rearguard action against the Norman invaders. These upstarts had conquered his land and robbed him of the patrimony that should have been his by right – an injustice he vowed to redress.

Ely in the English county of Cambridgeshire is today a pleasant cathedral city surrounded by endless vistas of flat and productive arable land. A thousand years ago, however, it was very different: it lay on an island entirely surrounded by fens. These boggy marshes, veined by innumerable streams, were lethal to travellers who did not know their secret paths, making the place an outlaws' heaven. And in the year 1070 a band of rebels, led by a charismatic Saxon nobleman, chose it as their base for a campaign of defiant resistance against England's new and foreign king.

Just four years earlier, the country had fallen to Duke William of Normandy, who had invaded across the English Channel and defeated its Saxon defenders at Hastings near the coast. William the Conqueror, as he would become known to history, set about consolidating his triumph methodically

and ruthlessly. All over the realm, people were forced to bow to his command or else see their lands taken from them and handed to new, Norman masters.

Inevitably, a bitter resentment brewed that flared repeatedly in local unrest. Many uprisings were put down with fire and the sword. By 1069 peace had settled over most of the land, yet in one area the flame of revolt still burned bright. That was in Ely, where it focused on a previously unknown local man named Hereward.

Contemporary records have little to say about him, though they do mention his name. The Domesday land registry shows that a man of that name did indeed hold estates in nearby Lincolnshire at the time of the Norman Conquest. And he also features in a single, long entry in the chief annals of the day, the *Anglo-Saxon Chronicle*.

The *Chronicle*'s report describes how, in the year 1070, "Hereward and his gang" colluded with Danish raiders to lead an attack on Peterborough Abbey, one of the richest in all England, in protest at the appointment of a new, Norman, abbot. In the course of the incident, buildings were set alight and the church was looted of its valuables. The Danes seem to have taken most of the plunder, for they subsequently retreated to their ships and were not seen again. Hereward made his way to Ely. There he was joined by many dissidents, including leading Saxon noblemen. When

The Norman cavalry proved decisive at the Battle of Hastings. Any successful resistance to William's forces was therefore best mounted from the more inaccessible reaches of the countryside. Scene from the Bayeux Tapestry, c.1070.

King William I besieged the island, the rebels held off all attempts to take it for nearly a year. When it eventually fell, Hereward and his men escaped.

Such was the bald historical record, but legend quickly took up the outlaws' cause. In the centuries after Hereward's death, many different accounts of his life were put on paper, some largely fictional, others perhaps drawing on local tradition. What is certain is that they catered to an abiding fascination with their subject; Hereward may have been defeated but he was not forgotten.

A Life in Legend

The story these works tell is of an adolescent hell-raiser who got into so many scrapes that his own father eventually banished him. The young man then set off on a series of adventures that seem to be straight from the tradition of courtly romance. In Scotland he supposedly tracked down and killed a bear, born of a princess and with a human intelligence, that had escaped from captivity. He then moved to Cornwall, where he rescued a nobly born lady from the unwelcome attentions of a giant. Calling in on Ireland, he fought in the wars of its rulers until word reached him that his father had died. Then he set sail for England, only to be driven off course by a storm and shipwrecked on the coast of Flanders, where he was at first imprisoned as a spy. While in the service of the local ruler, he met and married the wise and beautiful Turfrida, and also found a mount, Swallow, that was unmatched in courage and agility.

Hereward's Flemish entanglements kept him abroad until 1068. His homecoming turned out to be a bitter one, for he found that Normans had seized his father's lands. Worse, they had murdered his younger brother. Hereward arrived to find the young man's head skewered above the entrance to the family home.

From that moment on, he thought only of revenge. First, he killed all those responsible for his brother's death. Then, as news of that feat spread, he found himself the leader of a band of rebels. With them he launched his revolt.

With their own properties threatened by King William I, the monks of Ely finally betrayed Hereward. Here, a tonsured monk from a self-supporting community is reaping the harvest.

When the Normans were driven from the area, Hereward felt secure enough to travel back to Flanders to visit his wife. He returned within the year, his ranks now reinforced by some of Turfrida's Flemish relatives. It was presumably at this time that he staged his historic raid on Peterborough, though his biographers make little or no mention of it; no doubt, as monks, they had no desire to associate him with the looting of a religious building. Instead, they merely relate that rebels occupying the Isle of Ely contacted him to suggest joining forces against the common foe.

Hereward was only too happy to oblige. He took his men to Ely the long way round, by sea, escaping an ambush laid by the Earl of Warenne. They were welcomed on the island, with Hereward quickly recognized as a natural leader, despite the presence of several of the old Saxon ruling class, including Earl Morcar and Archbishop Stigand.

Before long the king decided that the Saxons' depredations could not go unpunished, and so the epic siege of the island got under way.

The Normans' first attempt at an open assault ended in disaster when a causeway they had built across the marshes collapsed under the weight of the soldiers, drowning many. William next resorted to cunning; his advisers persuaded him to employ the services of a sorceress, whose spells would, they promised, overcome the outlaws' resistance.

Leaked news that a fresh attack was being planned led to one of Hereward's most celebrated exploits. Determined to find out what was afoot, he disguised himself as a wandering potter and set off for the Norman camp. As luck would have it, he ended up spending the night in the same farmhouse as the witch, and heard her discussing her plans in French, which she wrongly assumed that he, as an ignorant Saxon, would not understand.

The next day he travelled on to the camp, where his resemblance to the famous Hereward was soon noted. He became an object of general curiosity, only managing to escape detection by swearing undying hatred of the rebels, who, he maintained, had robbed him of all he possessed. Even so, he was subjected to some savage teasing by the kitchen scullions, and after a time his patience snapped. Pulling out his sword, he struck down the worst of his tormentors, and then had to flee for his life with half the camp's garrison on his heels. One knight did eventually catch up with him, but was quickly disarmed and sent back to his fellows with the news that it was indeed Hereward who had been in their midst.

The information Hereward had gathered enabled the rebels to thwart the assault by hiding upwind of the attackers and, at a prearranged signal, setting fire to the reeds clogging the marshes. The Normans scattered in all directions before the blaze, and again many drowned. Among the first casualties was the witch, who had been set on a wooden siege-tower to cast her spells; leaping for safety from the top platform, she broke her neck.

Yet despite these triumphs, the Saxons' resistance was doomed, for the Norman grip on England was secure. Even though their refuge was amply stocked with food, they could not survive alone among their enemies forever. Eventually it was the monks of the Abbey of Ely who cracked. Learning that their mainland properties were to be confiscated, they secretly contacted William, promising to deliver Ely up to his forces. The king gladly accepted the offer.

Hereward was forewarned of the enemy's arrival. At first he wished to fight, but eventually was persuaded that resistance was hopeless. And so he and his men took to their boats and vanished from the island and from history. Legend has it that for a time they continued their struggle in the vast Bromswold woodlands east of Ely, before finally accepting the inevitable and making their peace with the king. Some accounts claim that Hereward was restored to his lands and died peacefully in his bed; but another tradition records that revengeful Norman rivals attacked and killed him in his own home. In this version, he resisted to the last, cutting down the man who had slain him even as he drew his dying breath.

Tales of Wild Edric

The Saxon resistance to the Norman invasion was not confined to the southeast of England. On the border with Wales another noble was dispossessed of his lands and took up arms against William's intruders – and in so doing entered legend as a hero beyond time.

In real life, Edric was a leading Saxon nobleman who fought for three years against the Normans and, after making a temporary peace with King William I, ended up losing all his lands. History then forgot him, but legend kept his memory alive. Medieval chroniclers claimed that, lost in the forest one night while out hunting, he abducted a fairy bride, only to lose her years later when he broke a promise never to mention her origins. In later times local people insisted that he did not die, but lived on with his followers in the lead-mines of Shropshire, riding forth at their head whenever England needed him. Another tradition even maintained that he bequeathed his sword to a great fish, which was sometimes seen in Bowmere Pool near the city of Shrewsbury with the weapon strapped to its side.

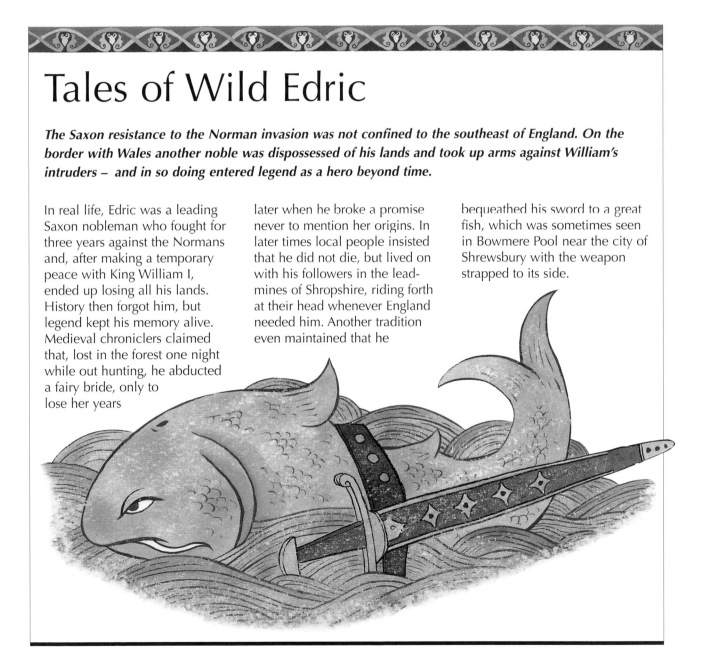

A Half-Forgotten Hero of Romance

Little remembered even in his home town today, Guy of Warwick was for seven centuries venerated as the ideal of the Christian knight, as ready to fight the enemies of the Lord as he was to rid the land of monsters or dragons.

Just beyond the northern suburbs of the modern English town of Warwick, a deserted mansion stands gauntly on a low bluff rising from the waters of the River Avon. In the grounds of this romantic ruin, still known as Guy's Cliffe, lies a small cave with some Saxon writing on the wall. This hermitage, according to legend, was the final abode of Guy of Warwick, hero of a cycle of Anglo-Norman epic romances, who devoted his final days to the service of God. In recent times his fame, which still shone brightly in the Romantic era 200 years ago, has gone into decline, but he was once considered to be the very model of medieval knight-errantry.

As told first in Anglo-Norman and then in various French and English versions in the twelfth and thirteenth centuries, the story started with the hero hopelessly in love. In Saxon times around the start of the eleventh century, the poems maintained, Guy, a son of the steward of the mighty Earl of Warwick, became enamoured of his lord's beautiful daughter, Felice. But she was far above his station, so in the finest knightly tradition he determined to win her love by performing feats of valour to impress her. He crossed the English Channel and won renown by rescuing the kidnapped daughter of the emperor of Germany.

Buoyed up by this success, he returned to Warwick and Felice, only to be rejected by her once more. So he set off again, this time for Constantinople to fight the Saracens. There he met their champion Coldran in single combat and slew him; and he subsequently dispatched the king of Tyre and even the Sultan himself. This time he returned to his homeland as the hero of all Christendom. Even Felice was impressed, and she at last consented to be his wife.

Yet she was not to enjoy his company for long. A vision of Christ came to Guy just days after the wedding, telling him that, having fought so long for the love of a woman, he should now turn his attention to God. So within forty days of the marriage Guy was off on his travels again, this time to go on a pilgrimage to the Holy Land. Distraught at his abrupt departure, Felice insisted on giving him a ring to wear at all times, telling him to think of her whenever it caught his gaze.

Needless to say, his passage was not a smooth one. There were giants to fight and fearsome adversaries to overcome. But once more Guy triumphed in all his ordeals, only to return to an England crawling with monstrous beasts that apparently only he was bold enough to hunt down. In Windsor Forest he killed a mighty boar; in Northumberland a serpent "black as any coal". The best-remembered of these valiant encounters was on Dunsmore Heath near Coventry, where he he slew a formidable creature known as the Dun

On the inside of a silver-gilt drinking vessel, Guy of Warwick is depicted killing a dragon, c.1300–50. Guy was a favoured English hero until well into the 19th century, heralded for saving the country from the Danes.

Jerusalem, as depicted in a medieval manuscript. Guy of Warwick answered a vision and proved his worthiness as a knight by embarking on a pilgrimage to the holy city. Although he dispatched adversaries on the way, he later renounced all worldly pursuits in favour of an ascetic existence devoted to God.

Cow. The property of a giant, it was itself of vast size and provided an inexhaustible supply of milk for all-comers until asked by a greedy old woman, who had already drawn a pailful, to fill her sieve also. This request so enraged the beast that it went on the rampage, killing and trampling people throughout the district until it was finally laid low by Guy.

Perhaps Guy's greatest exploit, however, was to rescue King Athelstan of England when he was besieged in the city of Winchester by Danes – a feat he achieved by killing their champion Colbrand. This incident seems to have been based on memories of an actual Danish invasion of southern England in the year 993, though in fact Winchester was saved from sacking at the time not by a feat of arms but the payment of money.

Having won the king's undying gratitude, Guy returned to Warwick but not to Felice, for he had determined to devote his last years uninterruptedly to God. So, without sending her word, he settled down to the life of a solitary hermit, going in rags each day to her house to beg for food without revealing his identity. Only when he realized he was dying did he send her the ring she had given him; and so the two, after so many years apart, were brought together at his death-bed.

Eustace the Marauding Monk

Not all tales required the fantastical embellishment of fact. One popular Old French saga fictionalized the career of a real-life outlaw whose own story was quite as strange as anything the romancers could have dreamed up.

Eustace the Monk was born Eustache Busquet, the son of a petty nobleman from Boulogne on France's Channel coast. Since his elder brother was set to inherit the family title and estate, his parents put him into a monastery. His natural craving, however, was for action and adventure – and it was not long before he found them.

When his father was murdered at the behest of a neighbouring nobleman in the course of a landholding dispute, Eustace abandoned his vows to seek justice from the region's ruler, the Count of Boulogne. He failed, but was offered a court appointment as a seneschal – a steward in charge of domestic arrangements – while the count went off to the wars. But his father's murderer, still harbouring a grudge against the family, laid false accusations of mismanagement against him. Convinced he would not get a fair hearing, Eustace quit the count's service and took to the woods.

As the romance tells the tale, the outlaw life suited him well. He spent his time outwitting and robbing the count's men and was a master of disguise. On one occasion he swapped clothes with a coal-deliverer to evade capture; then, having fooled his pursuers once, changed the coalman's garb for those of a potter, and did the same again.

There were slim pickings in the forest, however, and Eustace soon realized that there were richer rewards to be had at sea. At the time the English Channel was infested with pirates, and Eustace quickly made his mark among them. He evidently had leadership qualities too, for he soon had ships of his own under his command.

Eustace chanced his luck for many years, alternating between the patronage of English and French kings. At the Battle of Sandwich, however, he met his end. Eustace can be seen far right, being beheaded, in an engraving from a chronicle, c.1250.

Eustace and the Black Arts

While Eustace was portrayed as an outlaw hero, avenging wrongs that were visited upon his family, it was clear from many tales that he had a wicked streak. To explain Eustace's less savoury acts, it was claimed that in his youth he had studied the black arts in Spain.

"When he got back from Toledo," his biographer maintained, "there was no one in the kingdom of France who knew so much black magic or sorcery." Woe betide anyone who cheated him, for he felt obliged to get his own back by making them the butt of his new knowledge. So, when an inn-keeper's wife in the town of Montferrand overcharged him for his stay, he cast a spell on the tavern that caused all the bungs in the wine-barrels to fly out and all the guests to tear off their clothes. And when the abbot of his monastery near Boulogne refused him a share of a hearty repast, his response was to bring a pig's carcass that was hanging in the kitchen to life in the form of a hump-backed old hag. All the monks fled in terror, and Eustace helped himself to the meal.

When his depredations made the French coast too hot for him, he switched allegiance to King John of England, who was then at war with France. So it was with tacit royal backing that Eustace seized the Channel Island of Sark to serve as his headquarters. The fugitive from the law had become the ruler of his own small kingdom.

Nor was that the limit of his success. His attacks on French shipping won him such favour that King John awarded him estates in the county of Norfolk. He was even sent as a royal envoy to negotiate with his old enemy, the count.

But then the political situation changed to his disadvantage: John and the count made common cause. Fearing treachery, the pirate monk changed allegiance once more; now his ships roamed under French colours in search of English prey.

The switch must initially have seemed a smart move, for the French cause prospered while King John's reign stuttered to an end amid internal rebellion. When John eventually died in 1216, leaving the nine-year-old Henry III to inherit the throne, the French sensed a golden opportunity. Their ruler, Philip II Augustus, gathered a great fleet to invade England. Eustace suddenly found himself thrust centre stage as a leader, even being charged with carrying the king's son and co-regent, Louis the Lion, in person across to Kent.

In fact, though, the invasion proved to be his undoing. On a hot August day in 1217, his fleet was intercepted off Sandwich on the Kent coast and its flagship was seized. Eustace was found hiding in the hold of his vessel, recognized and dragged out on deck by his captors, who cut off his head and impaled it on a lance to dispirit the rest of the French fleet. And so Eustace died as he had lived; having made the sword his only law, he at last became its victim.

The Devil's Child

Inspired by a tale from their own history, Norman poets told of a cursed hero who devoted his life to escaping the diabolical inheritance that was his birthright. And when he had finally shaken off his past, he asked to take up arms once more.

While the popular romance of Eustace the Monk stuck relatively closely to the real events of an extraordinary career, the saga of Robert le Diable never had more than a tenuous link to historical actuality. His legend, drawing on the Faustian theme of a child born in answer to prayers to Satan, was first recounted in a romance of the late twelfth century, and later provided the subject for two fourteenth-century poems. Today, however, it is probably best remembered through Meyerbeer's nineteenth-century opera *Robert le Diable*, a Romantic-era piece that owes little more than its title to the traditional French story.

This tells how Robert was born to a childless Norman duke and grew up to be a prodigy of strength. But because of his satanic origins, he was cursed only to be able to use his powers for evil purposes. Yet the voice of his conscience refused to be stilled, and in time he came to repent the many terrible things that he had done during his life. Tormented by the curse that had been laid upon him, he went eventually to the pope himself for guidance, and the pontiff directed him to the one man who might save him – a hermit whose personal saintliness had given him dominion over the Devil and all his works.

The holy man agreed to help Robert, but on one condition: he must readily submit to a daunting set of penances. First he had to take a vow of silence; then he was made to feign insanity, taking his food from the mouth of a dog as a sign of self-abasement. And to test his humility, the fierce aristocrat who had once lorded it so proudly over the common people now had to deliberately provoke situations in which he became their butt, suffering disgrace and humiliation without retaliating in thought or deed.

Having willingly endured a series of harsh penances, Robert le Diable shed the infamy of his earlier warlike days. But when Rome was threatened by the Saracens, an angel appeared before him and implored him to take up arms once again. This angelic detail is from an 8th-century altar.

Finally, his self-imposed sufferings won him the grace that he had long craved. Freed of the satanic burden of pride, he willingly took up a post as court fool to the Holy Roman Emperor, Christendom's foremost secular defender. But his great strength was called on once more when Rome itself came under Saracen attack. At first Robert was unwilling to return to the ways of war, but when an angel descended to tell him his services were needed, he willingly took up the task.

Even so, he had eschewed arrogance, and so it was in the guise of an unknown knight that he rode out to do battle with the foe. Three times he ventured forth, and each time his efforts won the day for the Christian cause.

The fame of his deeds spread like wildfire through the ranks, and soon all Rome was on tenterhooks to learn the identity of the city's anonymous saviour. It was left to the emperor's own daughter, who had long secretly admired Robert, to see through his disguise. In one version of the story, the hero then received romantic compensation for his sufferings when he and the girl wed. But in another, no doubt preferred by the monks who wrote many such romances, he chose to seek his reward in Heaven, turning down the royal marriage to find salvation as a hermit instead.

A Case of Mistaken Identity

From early on, the legend seems to have become confounded in the public mind with memories of William the Conqueror's father, Duke Robert I of Normandy, himself known as "Robert le Diable". He won his diabolical reputation by reputedly poisoning his own brother in order to accede to power, and subsequently further shocked clerical opinion by giving away Church lands.

The only real link, though, between his career and that of his fictional namesake was that he, like many princes of the day, felt the need to do penance for his sins, and with that aim in mind set off on a pilgrimage to Palestine in 1035. He died of unknown causes in Anatolia on the return journey, no doubt suitably shriven. But so low was his reputation, at least among the God-fearing classes, that a rumour soon spread that he too had been poisoned, and thus dispatched prematurely to the eternal torments that his fictional namesake had so righteously avoided.

Beastly Beings

Wild men who lived like beasts beyond the pale of civilization held an enduring fascination for the medieval public.

Unkempt, hairy and surviving on raw meat or leaves, the wild man was the antithesis of the courtly knight. He lived like an animal in the wilderness, usually speechless and using only the most primitive tools. Yet sometimes misfortune in love could transform a knightly hero into just such a pitiable monster; such was the fate of Yvain in the Arthurian cycle and of Orlando, driven mad by love (see page 44).

In one sense, the wild man was a counterpart of the medieval outlaw, living like him in the depths of forests, places outside the reach of the law where the urbane ways of court no longer applied and strange changes could come over those who went astray.

The figure was celebrated by sculptors in the leaf-shrouded faces depicted in some Gothic churches. And it also formed part of an enduring worldwide tradition of man-beasts, stretching from Enkiddu, the shaggy giant of the Sumerian *Epic of Gilgamesh*, right up to modern-day accounts of backwoods Sasquatches and Himalayan Yetis.

The leaf-shrouded face was a favourite motif of Gothic sculptors. This wooden example adorns the ceiling of Norwich Cathedral in England.

A Banished Baron's Fight for Justice

Often thought of as a precursor of Robin Hood, Fulk FitzWarin came from a more aristocratic background, and his adventures harked back to an older tradition of knightly romance. His motivation, however, was justice, and the butt of his ire the same King John.

The real Fulk FitzWarin was a lord on England's marches with Wales in the bad days of King John at the start of the thirteenth century. Dispossessed of the family estate of Whittington in Shropshire after a lawsuit in the year 1200, he spent three years as an outlaw before receiving a royal pardon. He then lived peaceably until 1215, when he joined in the Barons' Revolt against John that ended when the king was forced to sign the charter of liberties known as Magna Carta. After John's death he again recovered Whittington, which he had lost a second time in the revolt, and lived on there to die in the mid-1250s, by which time he must have been well into his eighties.

He obviously made a great impression on his contemporaries, for after his death he became the subject of a verse romance, now lost. The story known today comes from a prose summary written around 1340 by a scribe in the city of Hereford.

The romance concentrates on Fulk's outlaw years, between 1200 and 1203. It traces the origins of his quarrel with John to a childhood incident in which the two squabbled over a game of chess. John crashed the board down on Fulk's head and was beaten for his pains. The future king's memory was long, and when he came to the throne in 1199 he took revenge by granting the manor of Whittington to another claimant. Outraged at the loss of the property, Fulk took to the woods to seek justice.

Although the *Romance of Fulk FitzWarin* draws on fact for this central theme, its account of Fulk's subsequent adventures plunges wildly into fantasy. The poet sends him to Scotland, Brittany, France and Spain on exploits that include rescuing a king's daughter from seven robber chiefs, killing a dragon that lives off human flesh, and fighting as a champion of the Saracens against a Christian opponent who turns out to be his own brother. After this last exploit he almost incidentally converts the Saracens to Christianity before returning to England to win back his inheritance from King John.

Such impressive feats were common currency in the knightly romances that delighted audiences in the early Middle Ages, and that were eventually to be satirized affectionately by Miguel de Cervantes in *Don Quixote*. More interesting in many ways are the relatively realistic incidents described when Fulk gets closer to home, which often predict, and in one or two cases directly parallel, tales that would later crop up in the Robin Hood cycle. One such event occurs when Fulk captures ten merchants travelling through a forest carrying cloth destined for King John. The outlaw helps himself to enough of the costly material to make rich garments for all his men, then feasts the burgesses and sends them on their way, instructing them to tell the king that Fulk FitzWarin thanks him for the fine vestments he has provided.

Other incidents recall the Eustace the Monk story in the predilection shown for disguises. At one point Fulk hears that the king is to go hunting in Windsor Forest, and prepares an ambush for him in the depths of the wood. After exchanging clothes with a passing collier, he meets the king and offers to lead him on a stag's trail, only to deliver him up to his own men, for like Robin Hood Fulk had a band of loyal retainers to support him in his struggle. He only releases the monarch after John has sworn to restore Fulk's inheritance

to him – an oath the king promptly breaks on his return to court. But after King John has been captured on a second expedition, Fulk secures his pardon, and this time the pledge is honoured – allowing Fulk to return, at last, to Whittington.

Stag Hunting, by Gaston Phebus, *c.*1387. Many forests, held as hunting preserves for royalty and the wealthy, provided the setting for social tensions and grievances. Fulk captured King John in the depths of the forest while he was hunting, but he released him after the king vowed to restore his inheritance.

Rhymes of Robin Hood

Champion of justice and friend of the poor, the best-known medieval outlaw may not have actually existed at all. But while his feats remain the stuff of legend, the world in which they took place was very real indeed.

The first datable reference to Robin Hood comes in William Langland's *Piers Plowman*, one of the great English poems of the Middle Ages. In it a clergyman representing Sloth says that he does not know his prayers well but he is familiar with "rhymes of Robin Hood". The "rhymes" Langland had in mind when he was writing in 1377 were almost certainly ballads, sung by minstrels in barons' halls as well as at fairs and other popular gatherings. The fact that Sloth could refer to them so familiarly suggests that they were already well-known to Langland and his readers by that time.

Almost all the original Robin Hood material comes from these ballads, half a dozen of which have been dated back to the fifteenth century or earlier. The longest, *A Little Gest of Robin Hood*, in fact seems to consist of three or four separate tales woven together to make a continuous whole. Between them, they already contain in essence the entire legend that was to be elaborated over the next six centuries.

Yet they also contain one or two surprises for modern readers. The Sheriff of Nottingham is the villain of the piece from the start and Sherwood Forest in Nottinghamshire is mentioned, but most of the action takes place in Barnsdale, a district of modern-day South Yorkshire about fifty kilometres to the north. Whoever composed the ballads seems to have had local knowledge of this region, for there are references to relatively obscure places – Sayles Plantation, Plumpton Park – that could hardly have been known to an outsider.

There are also gaps in the information that the ballads provide. Nowhere do they make it clear why Robin became an outlaw. Stories that he was a nobleman unjustly deprived of his lands belong to a later tradition. In the early ballads he is a yeoman – a small landholder not in service to any man – and proud of it.

Whatever may have led him to the forest, Robin lives there by poaching the king's deer and by robbing travellers who can afford to pay. He spells out his code of conduct quite clearly to his companions, telling them to show no mercy to law officers or to bishops and abbots – for at this time the Church was famously wealthy and unpopular with many ordinary people. But they are not to

Poet-balladeers, also known as troubadours or minstrels, exerted a profound influence on medieval poetry and literature, helping to preserve traditional stories and shape social attitudes. The first written reference to Robin Hood comes in the 14th century, but tales of his exploits date back further to the songs of travelling musicians, shown here in a 13th-century songbook.

The Growth of a Legend

Scholars still argue over whether Robin Hood was a historical figure or a being from myth.

One school of thought, first developed in the nineteenth century, insists that the origins of the Robin Hood legends lie in mythology. This view sees him as a forest sprite linked to the fairy known as Robin Goodfellow, another name for the Puck of Shakespeare's *Midsummer Night's Dream*.

But other scholars look to the early ballads and discover no evidence of any such esoteric associations. Instead they find earthy narratives with a clear social setting and a distinct geographical locale on the borders of Nottinghamshire and Yorkshire in north-central England. In their view the nature of the tales indicates that there must have once been a real Robin Hood, even if he has left no trace in the historical record and if his name has since become infused with legend. The search for candidates goes on. Some researchers have made claims for a "Robyn Hode", listed as a porter of the chamber of Edward II in 1324, but the date seems too late for the earliest ballads.

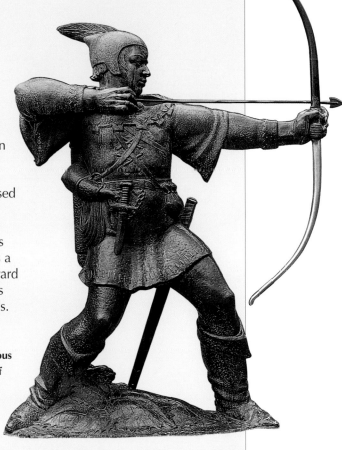

A statue of Robin Hood in his famous forest garb, from the English city of Nottingham. One theory suggests that his roots are mythological and not historically based at all.

harm any husbandman (peasant farmer). And Robin explicitly states: "Whoever helps a good yeoman/His friend then will I be."

Faithful Companions

Some familiar names form part of his band from the start. Little John features in several of the early ballads, and is in fact the real hero of *Robin Hood and the Monk*, possibly the earliest of them all. Will Scarlett also appears from the beginning, though under the name of Will Scathelocke, as does Much the Miller's son. Friar Tuck is first mentioned in a fragment of a play dating from about 1475. Interestingly, though, a bandit calling himself by that name had operated in the south of England almost sixty years before, and it is at least possible that this man – a chaplain, Robert Stafford – was the real-life original of the character in the stories.

As for Maid Marian, she seems to have first entered the Robin Hood canon during the sixteenth century, as part of the May Day festivities in which plays about the outlaw were a regular and popular feature. There is a separate French romance called *Robin and Marian*, in which Marian is a shepherdess and Robin is simply her true love, and it is possible that memories of this story may have got mixed up at some stage with the folk hero of Sherwood.

Some of the incidents in the ballads also seem to have travelled across stories. In one Robin exchanges clothes with a potter, just as both Hereward and Eustace the Monk had done before him. In this version he takes his wares to Nottingham market, where they attract the attention of the sheriff's wife, netting him an invitation to the castle. In the course of the tale he gets the chance to reciprocate the hospitality, for when he tells the sheriff that he knows Robin Hood, his host insists on being taken to Sherwood Forest to meet the outlaw. There Robin reveals his true identity and robs him of everything he has with him, courteously giving him in exchange a white steed as a gift for his wife. From his takings he gives the potter three times the value of his pots, so everyone except the sheriff ends up contented.

Not all the early ballads are as good-hearted. In *Robin Hood and the Monk*, the hero is betrayed while at prayer in church. As a reward for his treachery, the monk who informed on him is dispatched to London to inform the king that the famous outlaw has been caught. But he is waylaid en route by Little John and Much the Miller's son, who kill both him and his pageboy. They then swap clothes with their victims and journey on to court, where they are well received by the monarch and provided with letters instructing the Sheriff of Nottingham to send Robin Hood to London so the king can see him in person.

Armed with what in effect are release papers for the prisoner, the two return to Nottingham and are welcomed by the sheriff, who mistakes them for genuine royal messengers. That night, after dining well, they rescue Robin, killing his guard in

Like many medieval outlaws, Robin Hood was most at ease in woodland, where town folk might lose their way – and even their lives – and the king's laws were difficult to enforce. Today, Sherwood Forest in Nottinghamshire, seen below, is regarded as having been Robin's home, although various traditions have linked him with areas of England as far afield as Yorkshire in the north and Rutland further south.

Feats of archery were prominent in the Robin Hood tales, prowess with the bow being a skill found widely among England's social classes at the time. The longbow was in fact the national weapon and for a time regular practice was compulsory. English bowman illustrated in the *Luttrell Psalter, c.1340.*

doing so, and the three are safely back in Sherwood the following morning, when the sheriff wakes up to the embarrassing task of informing the king of the outlaw's escape.

The fragmentary ballad of *Robin and Guy of Gisborne* is even bloodier in tone. At one point Robin kills the man of that name and cuts off his head. He then disfigures the face so badly that no one could recognize it. The point is that he can then don the dead man's clothes and pass himself off as Guy, pretending that the severed head is that of Robin Hood.

Robin and the King

Some of the themes of these ballads crop up again in *A Little Gest of Robin Hood.* A corrupt churchman is discomfited and an honest but impoverished knight helped to save his inheritance; once more the Sheriff of Nottingham is an unwilling guest in Sherwood Forest, though this time at Little John's bidding. But the last part adds new matter to the legend by bringing the king of England himself to Sherwood Forest. The monarch – the ballad calls him only "Edward" without specifying which of the three early medieval rulers of England of that name it has in mind – turns the tables on the outlaws by adopting their own stratagem of disguise, dressing himself as a rich abbot ripe for robbing.

Sure enough, the trick works and the outlaws end up unwittingly kidnapping their sovereign. In a trial of strength with Robin, Edward soon shows his true mettle and the outlaw sees through his

disguise, falling to his knees reverently as he does so and humbly begging the king's forgiveness for all the wrong he and his men have done. Edward graciously pardons them, stipulating only that they must leave the greenwood and that Robin should enter his own service. Then he pays the outlaws the highest compliment possible by agreeing to don their own distinctive green livery to lead them out of the forest and back into society at large.

A Final Betrayal

And so the story might have ended, but the editor of the *Little Gest* felt compelled to add an epitaph about Robin's death. As he tells it, life in service did not suit the famous bandit, and he soon left court to return to his old greenwood ways. He lived a fugitive life in Barnsdale for another twenty-two years. Then as an old man he fell sick and went to Kirklees Abbey to be bled. But there he once more met betrayal. Although the prioress was of his own kin, she was also the lover of one of his enemies, and at this man's urging she determined to bleed him to death. By the time Robin realized what was afoot he was already weakened, though he still had the strength left to kill his foe. Then he fired a final arrow from the window, saying that he should be buried where it lay, before falling back dead.

Kirklees Abbey really existed, and a spot said to be Robin Hood's grave can still be found near its former site, lending extra verisimilitude to the legend. Yet whether or not Robin actually lived, it is certainly true that the world in which the ballads placed him, its social tensions and its irreverent attitudes, was real enough. And to judge from the tales' longevity, so was the need they supplied – for a people's hero, dedicated to robbing only the rich and to doing violence to none who did not richly deserve their fate.

Heroes for the People

Besides ordinary outlaws, there were rebels espousing more political causes. Coventry's Lady Godiva used femininity to achieve her aims, but William Tell is remembered in Switzerland as the bold and forthright hero of the struggle waged by the forest cantons for independence from their Austrian overlords.

In the early fourteenth century, when the Tell legend is set, Switzerland did not exist. The three cantons of Schweiz, Uri and Unterwalden that were to form its heart were feudal dependencies of the Holy Roman Emperor, though in practice they enjoyed a large measure of independence. That situation was challenged by the Austrian Habsburgs who sought to bring the Swiss to heel. As a result, the three cantons formed the Swiss Confederation to fight for their rights; and it was from this alliance that the future nation was to grow.

Tell's story is inextricably enmeshed with the founding of this confederation. It tells how the hated Governor Gessler set his hat up in the marketplace of Altdorf, the chief town in the canton of Uri, and ordered all citizens to bow to it as a symbol of Austrian rule. When Tell refused to obey, Gessler had him seized. Hearing that he was a fine shot, he ordered him to dislodge an apple from the head of his young son Walter, who was with him. Tell obeyed and split the apple in two.

Noticing that Tell had taken a second bolt from his quiver, Gessler insisted on knowing why. When Tell confessed that it was to kill him if any harm had befallen his son, the governor gave orders for him to be imprisoned in the castle at Kussnacht on the opposite shore of Lake Lucerne.

But while the prisoner was being transported across the lake, a high wind blew up. Fearing for his own life, Gessler gave orders that Tell should be unbound and given the tiller, for no one else could handle the boat in the storm. The hero brought it safely almost to land, then leaped to his freedom with a mighty bound, sending the vessel scudding back out among the waves. The point where the incident supposedly took place is known to this day as Tell's Leap.

As patriotic Swiss historians subsequently told the story, the indignation roused by Gessler's treatment of Tell, together with many other abuses of power, inspired a general uprising of the people on 1 January 1308. The movement proved irresistible, and reached fruition when the Swiss routed the Austrian army at Morgarten in 1315. As for Gessler, he was dispatched by Tell himself, who ambushed him near Kussnacht Castle.

Later historians, however, have suggested that almost all of the Tell story was made up. There is no contemporary evidence that a freedom fighter of that name ever existed, and the earliest version of the story dates from at least 150 years after the events it describes.

Yet like all good legends the tale of Tell has taken on a life of its own. The German dramatist Friedrich von Schiller took it as the theme of one of his best-known plays in 1804, and in 1829 Rossini turned it into an opera. Not only in Switzerland but around the world, the story is too firmly entrenched as an exemplum of resistance to oppression to be dislodged easily.

An early 16th-century decorated sporting crossbow from Germany. The doubtful accuracy of such weapons lends the William Tell story a major part of its dramatic tension.

A Woman's Ride for Justice

One famous English tale relates how it took a lady to make common cause with the people. In an age when women had little political power, she used the only weapon available to her – her beauty.

There really was a Lady Godiva – more correctly, Godgifu or "Gift of God" – though there is no contemporary record of the ride through the city of Coventry for which she became famous. The earliest record of the event comes in the chronicle of Roger of Wendover, writing more than 150 years later, who gives the date as 1057.

As he told the story, Godiva was constantly pestering her husband, Earl Leofric of Mercia, to reduce the taxes on the people of Coventry, where the two had jointly founded a monastery in 1043. Tiring of her ceaseless pleading, he eventually told her he would do as she wished – but only if she was prepared to ride naked through the town's busy marketplace. No

doubt he intended merely to put an end to her cajolery, but if so he misjudged his wife. For she duly did as he required, taking care that her nakedness was covered by the long flowing hair that was fashionable for women at the time.

The detail that all townsmen were ordered to stay indoors behind shutters for her ride was a later addition, as was the story that one, Peeping Tom, disobeyed and was struck blind for his effrontery. But there is at

least some evidence that Coventry really did pay little tax in the early Middle Ages – an enquiry carried out in the late thirteenth century established that the only toll in force there was one on horses.

THE LORE OF HUNTING

For the medieval nobility, hunting was a pastime that enabled courtiers to play out their warrior roles in peacetime against a background of tamed and gentle nature. For many ordinary people, however, the activity became a symbol of tyranny. In England, for example, the hunting grounds were lands appropriated by Norman lords, with laws curtailing people's traditional rights such as gathering firewood or grazing pigs. From these conflicting perspectives two distinctive traditions grew: a figurative art that captured the court at leisure, civilized within the forest; and a rich seam of legends that described figures such as Robin Hood or Fulk FitzWarin feasting on their despotic king's deer – living as outlaws in the woods, true only to their own fair and honourable codes.

Left: Scenes of hunting and harvesting carved in a 12th-century ivory panel. The greatest resource offered by forests was wood, which was used for kindling, making furniture or as joists for housing. Norman forest laws, however, meant that ancient rights of gathering and hunting in many places were taken away from ordinary English people.

Below: The New Forest, in Hampshire, was the first area of land to be subject to forest law and became King William I's favourite hunting ground. The legislation was highly emotive because woodland areas had been places of great industry, where pigs were grazed, trees felled and charcoal burned to feed the iron furnaces of nearby towns.

Left: This cap would have been placed over the head of a nobleman's hawk and only removed when the time came to pursue the quarry. Hawking carried great prestige in both material and symbolic terms – for not only was the sport expensive but it also showed the keeper's mastery over animals.

Left: Hawking scene from the *Tres Riches Heures du Duc de Berry* by the Limbourg brothers, 15th century. Falconry was more than an elaborate leisure pursuit of the nobility. Its clearly defined rituals celebrated the highly ordered nature of medieval society.

Below: While not employing the elaborate finery of their aristocratic overlords, commoners were proficient at hunting with dogs, shown here engaging in a boar hunt, in a scene from a 14th-century manuscript.

POKING FUN AT THE POWERS-THAT-BE

The Middle Ages were in many ways a time of tight social control. The different orders of society were rigidly separated and each had clearly defined duties and responsibilities. In the moral sphere, the Church kept a close watch on people's behaviour and was quick to condemn any deviance.

Yet there was always another side to the times – one that railed against authority and took delight in making fun of rules and conventions. Socially, this anarchic tendency found expression in the Feast of Fools, held around New Year's Day each year, in which Church rituals were parodied and pretend bishops or popes elected. In later years there were the Abbots of Unreason and Lords of Misrule chosen in universities and law schools to preside over Christmas festivities. Politically, this rebellious spirit took a violent turn in the many peasant uprisings and millenarian movements of the day.

The satiric spirit also found a natural home in the arts. One route was via the poetry of the *goliards*, bohemian students and clerics whose works hymning wine, women and song are best remembered today through the composer Carl Orff's settings in the *Carmina Burana*. Another was through drama. Some of the first secular plays staged were the *soties* of France, short pieces performed at carnival time poking fun at human foolishness. Germany had its *Fastnachtspiele*, often lampooning greedy clerics and corrupt officials.

So it was hardly surprising that the same satirical spirit should also make itself felt in the folk tradition. It expressed itself in the earthy humour of Till Eulenspiegel (see page 128); also in animal fables, which in the saga of Reynard the Fox developed into a parody saga neatly reversing the self-sacrificing virtues of the heroes of the Charlemagne cycle (see page 33). Those same champions, Roland among them, also came in for burlesque treatment in *The Pilgrimage of Charlemagne*, a mock-epic from the twelfth century.

Irreverent tales of Dame Fortune and her gifts turned *Fortunatus* into a late-medieval best-seller. And folktales in a similar vein were shaped into great literature by Boccaccio, whose masterpiece the *Decameron*, like the other works, drew much of its vitality from the story-telling tradition that flourished across the continent.

Opposite: A sculpture of a mouth-pulling figure, from York Minster, England. Such irreverent imagery was found throughout Europe.

Below: The fool or jester was a key figure at medieval courts, helping to deflate pomposity. Border detail from a 13th-century manuscript.

113

The Ruses of Reynard the Fox

A spiritual cousin of Africa's Ananse and America's Brer Rabbit, Reynard was an animal trickster who got his way by cunning. But the mock-epics detailing his adventures overlaid the stories with a distinctive gloss of social satire.

Animal tricksters were the original anti-heroes of medieval folklore. Far from being virtuous and chivalric they were by turns gluttonous, self-serving and morally reprehensible – yet they still attracted their audience's sympathy for their energy and quick wits. This was never more true than of the character of Reynard the Fox, whose persistent wrong-doings, interrupted by brief moments of repentance, fascinated people across much of Europe throughout the Middle Ages.

Many of the Reynard stories drew on folktales that were ages old, but they seem first to have been written down in the Flanders-Germany border region in the tenth or eleventh century. Their popularity spread rapidly, and by the thirteenth century there were versions in many European languages, including the famous French *Roman de Renart* and the German *Fuchs Reinhard*, which was to be updated by the great Goethe 500 years later. In England, translations appeared in the early sixteenth century.

Over the years many sub-plots were added, including the story of the strutting cock Chanticleer, lured through vanity into the fox's mouth, which Geoffrey Chaucer included in *The Canterbury Tales*. But the main body of the narrative focused on Reynard's trial before a Council of Animals presided over by King Noble the Lion, the epitome of the just (if sometimes credulous) medieval ruler.

The parallels with the human world were an essential part of the tales'

Detail from a 13th-century manuscript of *Roman de Renart*. The story is believed to have originated in Flanders around the 10th or 11th century, but it soon spread throughout the continent.

A Menagerie of Magical Animals

In bestiaries as in fables, medieval people interpreted animal behaviour as a reflection of their own. These zoos between book covers also sought to draw morals about the ways of God and humankind.

Exquisitely illustrated with a fanciful illumination, each entry in a bestiary (see pages 132–133) would typically start with a Biblical quotation before going on to report some odd detail about a given creature from which the author would then draw a moral. Lion cubs, for instance, were said to be born dead and only brought to life after three days when their father breathed on them, just as God the Father brought Christ to life on the third day.

Creatures from classical mythology were especially popular. Satyrs, sphinxes and centaurs, for example, were all featured, as was the phoenix, which was credited with casting itself into flames to be born again – usually interpreted as an allegory of the death and rebirth of Christ.

One legendary creature that had a particular appeal was the unicorn, whose single horn was thought to have the power to purge poisons. Another story maintained that unicorns could only be captured by virgins, giving themselves up willingly to be suckled at their breasts.

A young woman with a unicorn from a 15th-century manuscript, *Livre des Symples Medicines*. Unicorns were of ancient origin and considered to have magical powers.

appeal, permitting story-tellers to poke satirical fun at the feudal society around them. Part of the joy of the Reynard cycle for medieval audiences must have lain in the shock of recognition as they glimpsed institutions they knew dressed up in unfamiliar animal guise.

As the animals gathered in a conclave before their sovereign, one subject quickly came to dominate all their discussions: the misdeeds of Reynard, who alone of the beasts had not deigned to attend. It seemed that almost everyone had a complaint to make about him: Isegrim the wolf, whose wife he had insulted; Wackerlos the dog, whose sausage he had stolen; Lampe the hare, whom he had almost killed. Only one animal spoke out in his favour, and that was his nephew, Grimbart the badger. Moved by family loyalty, he effectively showed that Isegrim and Wackerlos had both been quite as guilty of greed as Reynard. As for the hare, Grimbart maintained, his uncle had only meant to chastise him for laziness while teaching him to sing his psalms.

Grimbart spoke eloquently, and had almost swayed the court in Reynard's favour when a dramatic eruption undid all his efforts. Chanticleer the cock appeared bearing the mortal remains of a hen. It seemed that when the dogs keeping guard over his farmyard had left to attend the council, Reynard had struck. Disguised as a monk, he had entered the yard and killed all but five of the

115

cock's brood, shamelessly violating the royal truce that had always attended such peaceful gatherings.

King Noble was outraged at this offence against his authority and decided on instant action. He sent Bruin the bear to Reynard's estate of Malpertuis to arrest the miscreant. But the fox was equal to the challenge, playing on his would-be captor's weaknesses to turn the tables. Pretending to go willingly, he managed to divert his guard to a peasant's yard, where a half-split tree trunk was held apart by wedges. He then persuaded Bruin that there was honey in the hole. When the bear's muzzle was firmly in the crack he whipped out the wedges, trapping him. Bruin's howls soon brought the peasant, who beat him black and blue before he was finally able to break free. By then his prisoner was long gone back to his wife and family in Malpertuis.

The next royal messenger had no better luck. Reynard sent Tibert the cat mousing through a hole in a barn wall, straight into a trap the fox knew was waiting on the other side; he too was lucky to escape with his life. This time King Noble's anger knew no bounds. Seeing this, Reynard's friend Grimbart thought it best to go himself, aiming to use his influence with Reynard to persuade him to obey the monarch.

When Reynard heard that a personal appearance at court was probably his last chance, he agreed to go. His arrival caused a sensation. So many charges were brought against him that he was quickly found guilty and sentenced to death. Desperately seeking a way out of his predicament, he begged for a chance at least to confess his sins, and King Noble generously granted his request.

The story of Reynard the Fox spread throughout Europe and was often used to illustrate lessons in morality. This wood carving from Bristol Cathedral in England shows men beating a greedy Bruin the bear whose head is stuck in a split tree trunk. The mischievous Reynard looks on, enjoying the results of his cunning.

Realizing his wits were his last resort, Reynard rapidly began inventing lies to save his skin. Faking contrition, he insisted that his greatest fault was to have become involved in a plot to dethrone and kill King Noble. He took care to implicate all his chief accusers, including Bruin, Isegrim and Tibert, in the conspiracy, and maintained that they had amassed a huge sum of money to finance their intrigue. He promised to reveal where this treasure lay if the king would spare his life. All he asked was to be sent on pilgrimage to Rome so that he could atone for all the wrong he had done.

Persuaded by his silver tongue, King Noble immediately had Isegrim and the others flung into prison. What was more, he not only gullibly consented to Reynard's request to go on a pilgrimage, but he dispatched Bellyn the ram and Lampe the hare to see him on his way. Needless to say, the crafty fox had barely left court before he had killed and eaten Lampe. In a gruesome twist he hid the crime from Bellyn, fooling the ram into returning to court with a wallet that he insisted contained secrets for the king. In fact, Lampe's head was inside. Furious at being tricked, King Noble ordered Bellyn's execution.

But his anger with Reynard was even greater, and he quickly had him dragged back to court to face justice. This time things looked black indeed for the trickster, but he did not despair – he would simply have to be craftier than ever. In his defence, he spelled out all the many services he had done the king over the years, and then made an emotional appeal calculated to touch the heart of a devout medieval monarch. Let God himself decide between him and his enemies, he proclaimed – and he then heroically declared that, despite his smaller size, he was willing to meet his chief accuser, Isegrim the wolf, in trial by combat.

Noble the Lion assented, and the showdown was arranged. Reynard, of course, was not the most courageous of animals and it goes without saying that he had a ruse in mind. Before the fight, he shaved off his fur and had himself rubbed all over with butter. When the contest began, he kicked dust in Isegrim's face to blind his opponent. And even when the wolf did manage to close with him, he could get no purchase on his slippery opponent. And so Reynard was able to get the upper hand and emerge as the winner.

To gain favour with the crowd, he asked for Isegrim's life to be spared, and the wolf slunk away to lick his wounds in disgrace. Meanwhile Reynard, having proved his innocence, became the toast of the court. He was even offered a post as a privy councillor – and so in the human world too, the authors of the fable implied, many a man who had risen to high office owed his ascension to quick wits more than to honesty or merit.

The Weasel and the Baby

Another animal that was considered sly was the weasel. Thought at the time to be venomous, it could also show very human emotions – or so one Welsh tale claimed.

According to Gerald of Wales, a man found a weasel's nest inside a sheepskin in his house in Pembroke and carefully removed it with the weasel's young still inside. When the mother returned and found her litter gone, her grief was so great that she determined to take revenge. So she went to the jug of milk set aside for the man's infant son and, raising herself on her hind legs, spat poison into it.

The man saw her doing so, and hurried to put the sheepskin back in its place. When the mother weasel saw that no harm had been done to her young, she squeaked with delight, then rushed back to the jug and knocked it over so that all the milk was spilt. In her gratitude at the return of her own offspring, she was determined that no harm should come to the human child.

The Pilgrimage of Charlemagne

Known from a single surviving Anglo-Norman copy, the mini-epic describing Charlemagne's pilgrimage to Jerusalem and subsequent voyage to Constantinople is unique in its burlesque tone as well as its naive delight in Eastern wonders.

Scholars date the *Pilgrimage of Charlemagne* to the second half of the twelfth century, and it now seems very much a creation of its time. Two crusades had already drawn thousands of fighting men from all over Europe to the Holy Land, and the travellers' tales of those who returned stimulated a popular fascination with all things Eastern. Yet while the crusaders' accounts of oriental marvels stirred the admiration of those who heard them, they also inspired a degree of envy. Almost like travelling sports fans today, ordinary people in the West felt the need to assert the superiority of their own culture over that of the foreigners. These conflicting attitudes of awe and of contention come over strongly in the work, which seems to have been aimed at a popular audience perhaps gathered for the French festival of St Denis, a time of general merriment and ribald good humour.

Certainly the work gets under way in the Church of St Denis, north of Paris. The anonymous author describes the great Charlemagne preening himself before the assembled lords and barons. Taking his wife Bertha aside to ask her if she has ever seen or heard of a more splendid monarch, he is more than a little peeved when she, showing an unexpected flash of independence, replies that indeed she has. Furious at the unexpected blow to his self-esteem, the ruler commands her under threat of losing her head to tell him who she has in mind. Already fearing the consequences of her rashness, she confesses that she was thinking of Hugh, the ruler of the Byzantine Empire.

Still angry, Charlemagne decides there and then that he must go east to find out if she is telling the truth. So he summons his twelve paladins – among them Roland, Oliver and Archbishop Turpin (see pages 34–39) – and commands them to accompany him first to Jerusalem to visit the various holy places and then on to Hugh's capital of Constantinople.

The Wonders of Jerusalem

Arriving at their initial destination, they go immediately to the Church of the Holy Sepulchre, where they commit unwitting sacrilege by sitting down for a rest on thirteen seats, not realizing that these are the chairs used by Jesus and the Apostles at the Last Supper. They are reprimanded by the Patriarch of

Gold and enamel reliquary, *c.*13th century, used to contain sacred objects or relics. The golden casket Charlemagne brought home from Constantinople was said to have held, among other marvels, Christ's shroud and hairs from St Peter's beard.

Jerusalem, who nonetheless welcomes them when he hears that they have come for the love of God. At Charlemagne's request, the holy man gives them a whole casketful of holy relics to take back to France: Christ's shroud, hairs from St Peter's beard, a drop of the milk the Virgin Mary fed to the baby Jesus and other wonders. Charlemagne has them all fastened up in a splendid gold reliquary, and many miracles of healing subsequently happen in their presence.

The Magnificence of Constantinople

Charlemagne and his knights remain in Jerusalem for four months, before deciding that the time has come to put the queen's remarks about Emperor Hugh to the test. Then, taking cordial leave of the Patriarch of Jerusalem, they set out for Constantinople and the multiple splendours of the Byzantine Empire.

These turn out to be even more magnificent than they could have imagined. Their first sight of the city is of an orchard planted with pines and laurels in whose shade 20,000 knights, dressed in silk and white ermine, are relaxing over games of chess or backgammon, or else dallying with their lovers. They find Hugh, oddly, engaged in ploughing, though in no ordinary way; the monarch sits on a golden throne drawn by two mules, and the plough itself is also of gold. Charlemagne is particularly impressed to note that he leaves it unattended to accompany his unexpected guests back to the palace, but Hugh assures him there is no need to worry, for theft is unknown in his lands.

The palace itself turns out to be a marvel in its own right, for it is built around a central pillar that permits it to revolve gently in the breeze. As it turns, the wind catches a statue of two children holding horns of white ivory, and then begins to make gentle music. While Charlemagne's men are admiring these wonders, a storm blows up, setting the whole building spinning like a top. The knights all collapse in a heap.

That night they are feasted by their host, dining on venison, cranes and peppered peacocks.

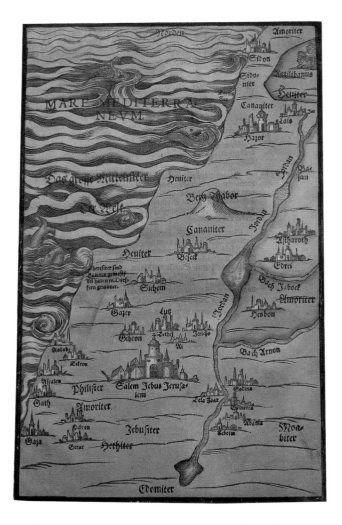

Medieval map of Jerusalem showing the major sites of the Holy Land. The monsters rising from the sea reinforce the idea that crusades were not only a chance to earn divine approval but a means of encountering strange and wonderful adventures.

They also drink rather too much wine, so by the time they are shown to their communal bedchamber, with its copper couches sheathed in silken sheets, they are in boastful mood. What they do not realize is that Hugh has hidden a spy in the room to learn if their intentions towards his kingdom are friendly.

In their drunken state, they pass the time in a bragging match. At Charlemagne's urging, each knight thinks up increasingly unlikely feats to achieve, mostly at the expense of their host and his realm. So Roland promises to blow a horn-blast so loud it will cleave in all the doors in the city, while

Guillaume d'Orange says he will take a great gold-and-silver sphere that ornaments the palace and roll it through the building like a bowling-ball. Ogier the Dane offers to pull out the central pillar and bring the whole structure crashing down, while Lord Bernard goes one further, proposing to divert a nearby river to flood the city. As for Oliver, who has been exchanging surreptitious glances with the emperor's beautiful daughter seated across the dinner table, he proclaims ribaldly that he will make love to the girl 100 times in a single night.

Medieval fresco of an angel. When Charlemagne's roistering knights seek assistance after being commanded to carry out their drunken boasts, an angel appears to help them – and chaos ensues.

All this the spy duly reports back to Emperor Hugh, who is not unnaturally upset by his guests' boorishness. Summoning them before him, he casts their own words back at them and asserts that they must perform the deeds they boasted of – or else lose their heads.

Things look black for the braggarts, but they still have one recourse: prayer. Charlemagne orders them all down on their knees before the chest of relics. Their pleas are dramatically answered when an angel appears to reprove them for their drunken raillery – but also to promise them divine aid in carrying out their tasks. They return to the hall and agree to Hugh's terms.

With celestial help, they in fact wreak so much havoc that only three of the feats get attempted before Hugh agrees to call the whole project off. First Oliver disappears with the emperor's daughter, who has fallen hopelessly in love with him; and even though he only manages to prove his virility about thirty times, she is more than happy to vouch that he has fulfilled his boast to the letter. Then Guillaume rolls his sphere to

such effect that he knocks down forty walls, half wrecking the palace. The last straw comes when Bernard successfully diverts the river, threatening the whole city with disaster. Hugh takes refuge in a high tower, where he laments mightily, crying out that that he would willingly become Charlemagne's vassal if only he could undo the harm so far wrought.

Hearing the ruler's desperate words, Charlemagne graciously assents, and the Byzantine emperor duly pledges his allegiance. Charlemagne's paladins then agree that there can be no doubt that he truly is the more splendid monarch. Then the knights take their leave to return home, Oliver rather unchivalrously spurning the Byzantine princess's plea to accompany them.

Back in France, the royal party return to St Denis, where the enterprise began. Queen Bertha casts herself at her husband's feet, bewailing her temerity, and he graciously forgives her. And so the story ends in triumph for the knights, which – given their uncouth behaviour on the way – is probably more than they really deserve.

With its exotic settings and improbable adventures, the *Pilgrimage of Charlemagne* has something of the flavour of the wonder tales of the *Arabian Nights*, though with a sharper topical edge. It may well be that, like those stories, it was intended for public recitation, when its bawdy humour and wary attitude towards foreigners would no doubt have helped carry an audience. That, too, might explain its familiar attitude towards Charlemagne and his paladins; even though they may act crassly, they are nonetheless local champions on an away trip, and the audience's identification with them is never in doubt.

In Search of Wondrous Lands

Tales of exotic places and their bizarre inhabitants enthralled people all across Christendom. But some of the most fantastic accounts of the far-off world were no more than elaborate works of fiction.

Although most people spent all their lives close to home, long-distance travel was nonetheless a feature of medieval life. The growth of commerce encouraged merchants to voyage ever further in search of trade. The crusades provided a huge stimulus, attracting thousands of campaigners to make the long trek east towards the Holy Land. And, in the thirteenth century, the peace following the Mongol conquest of Asia opened a corridor for the Venetian merchant Marco Polo, as well as a handful of Western monks, to voyage even further afield, to China and India.

Such real-life odysseys inspired some authors to flights of fantasy to please an audience avid for news of foreign lands. One of the most popular books of the fourteenth century was the *Travels of Sir John Mandeville* – actually a work of fiction concocted from real-life travellers' tales by a French writer who probably never even left home himself.

Even more audacious was a letter sent to the pope and some of Europe's rulers, supposedly from Prester John – a fabled Christian king believed to rule a kingdom in eastern Asia. In it the imaginary monarch boasted of the magnificence of his realm, whose seventy-two provinces housed "men with horns, men with eyes before and behind, centaurs, fauns, satyrs, giants and Cyclopses", not to mention a race of cannibalistic warriors who, with the king's permission, would kill and eat the empire's enemies. The pope was impressed enough by the document to send his physician eastwards with a reply. The envoy was never seen again.

Strange dog-human creatures from the early 15th-century *Livre des Merveilles* ("Wonders of the World").

Dame Fortune's Fickle Gift

A popular German tale of the late Middle Ages told how a young adventurer was given inexhaustible wealth by Dame Fortune – but far from being a fount of happiness the gift turned out to be a very mixed blessing indeed.

The story of Fortunatus enjoyed widespread popularity throughout medieval Europe. Its complicated, sometimes convoluted plot described how Fortunatus, the son of a wealthy wastrel from Famagusta in Cyprus, set out to make his own way in the world. After a series of adventures he ended up lost and penniless in a forest in Brittany, where he came across a fine lady who suddenly appeared as if from nowhere. Introducing herself as Dame Fortune, she offered him a choice: he could have wisdom, wealth, beauty and good health or a long life as a gift. He settled for riches, so she gave him a magical purse which would always have ten gold coins in it, and which would last for his lifetime and for that of his children.

The results of his choice were not all good. The very first time he used the purse, to buy a pair of horses coveted by the earl who owned the forest, he was taken for a thief and put in prison.

Buying his way out of gaol, he set off on a picaresque progress across Europe. He finally returned to Cyprus and married a count's daughter who bore him two sons, Ampedo and Andolosia. But some years later, Fortunatus got the urge to travel again, this time finding his way to Alexandria in Egypt. There he learned that the Sultan had another magical device: a hat that took the wearer wherever he wanted to be. Finding a pretext to try it on, he wished himself back to Cyprus with it.

Fortunatus used the two treasures for the rest of his life, and before dying passed on their secrets to his sons. Ampedo, a stay-at-home, had little use for them, but Andolosia set off on a round of exploits that took him to England and a troubled romance with a royal princess. When he finally returned to Cyprus he was imprisoned by two noblemen who had become envious of his wealth. They tortured him and discovered the secret of the magic purse. Meanwhile Ampedo, convinced the gifts could never bring happiness, had burned the wishing hat, dying soon afterwards.

Andolosia's ordeal at the hands of his kidnappers ended in his murder. The nobles got little reward for their crime, for the purse's magic was only vouchsafed for Fortunatus and his children, and with both of them dead it lost its potency. Robbed of the hoped-for riches, the killers quickly fell out; arrested, they confessed their wrong-doing and were sentenced to be broken on the wheel. And so the work arrived at its moral: that Fortunatus would have done better to have chosen wisdom than wealth, which causes quite as many problems as it solves.

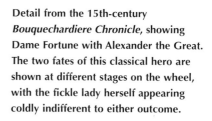

Detail from the 15th-century _Bouquechardiere Chronicle_, showing Dame Fortune with Alexander the Great. The two fates of this classical hero are shown at different stages on the wheel, with the fickle lady herself appearing coldly indifferent to either outcome.

A Faithful Wife Vindicated

One story of changing fortunes from Giovanni Boccaccio's **Decameron** *told of a wife's revenge on the man who had wronged her. And although it took several years to enact it nonetheless tasted sweet.*

When Bernabo of Genoa boasted of the fidelity of his wife Zinevra, his fellow-merchant Ambrogiuolo wagered him 5,000 florins that he could seduce her – for, he argued, no woman was chaste. Then he cheated to win the bet. He had himself carried into her chamber concealed in a chest. Emerging at night when she was asleep, he was able to note enough details of the room and of her own uncovered charms to convince Bernabo that she had indeed been unfaithful. Furious, he paid up the money, then gave orders that his wife be killed.

But the servant deputed to do the deed had not the heart for murder. Instead he let her go. Disguised as a boy, she found her way to Egypt and took service with the Sultan, rising to a position of authority in his court.

Then one day her betrayer Ambrogiuolo came to Egypt on a trading venture. Recognizing some former objects of hers among his merchandise, she wormed the story of his duplicity out of him. Using a stratagem to draw Bernabo from Italy, she summoned both before the Sultan and then, under threat of torture, forced Ambrogiuolo to reveal the truth.

Bernabo was overcome with guilt, bemoaning the terrible wrong he had done his

wife. At that point Zinevra revealed her true identity, and the two were reconciled. As for Ambrogiuolo, the Sultan sentenced him to death: covered in honey and tied to a post in the sun, he was left to the flies and mosquitoes.

Wise Men and Magi

Science had its roots in the medieval period, but people tended to view those who dabbled in it as wizards and sorcerers. Some of the practitioners even found their way into legend for the mighty wonders which rumour claimed they could work.

At a time when higher education was in the hands of the Church, it took courage for students to pursue fields of knowledge that did not have the stamp of official approval. But in the intellectual ferment of the times many did so. One of the first was a Scottish scholar and mathematician by the name of Michael Scot. Today he is remembered by scholars for his translations of Aristotle into Latin from Arabic and Hebrew. In his time, though, this innovative thinker, who studied in most of the great universities of Europe and for a time was employed by the pope himself, was best known as a wizard. And in his later years, when he came under the patronage of the free-thinking Emperor Frederick II in Sicily, he did indeed devote his time to the study of astrology, on which he wrote three treatises, and of alchemy, seeking to transmute base metals into gold.

Such activities were very much in keeping with the tone of the Sicilian court. Frederick himself was rumoured to have conducted bizarre experiments. To discover whether the soul existed, he had a condemned convict drowned in a barrel and watched carefully for any escaping emanation; failing to spot one, he concluded it did not. To settle an argument about whether language was inborn, he entrusted a group of newly born orphans to the care of deaf-mute nurses on an otherwise uninhabited island. That trial came to an end when plague killed all the participants.

Science and Superstition

In such a febrile environment, it was maybe not surprising that amazing rumours started to circulate about Scot too. People claimed that he rode a demon in the shape of a black horse and could make the bells of

A 15th-century engraving of a master and his two apprentices practising alchemy, searching for the ultimate secret of turning base metals into gold.

Notre Dame Cathedral in Paris ring from hundreds of kilometres away merely by waving a wand. Belief in his magical powers was only strengthened by a story that did the rounds after his death. Supposedly he had prophesied that he would die from a blow to the head, and to protect himself had taken to wearing a steel helmet at all times. But on the fateful day he took it off as a mark of respect when accompanying the emperor to church – and was promptly killed by a falling brick that cracked his skull.

Today Scot is best remembered for his work in reviving classical learning, helping to pave the way for the Renaissance. But in those early days, even the ancient masters were viewed through a prism of superstition. In particular the Roman poet Virgil, author of the *Aeneid*, gained a reputation as a necromancer, perhaps because of his memorable description of Aeneas's visit to the underworld in that work. People said that he had constructed a row of bronze statues representing the gods of the nations conquered by Rome, and had put a bell in the hands of each that rang whenever rebellion was brewing in that province. Others claimed he made a statue that could pronounce the names of criminals and wrong-doers.

Friar, Scientist and Magician

Another great medieval scientist, Roger Bacon, passed on in his writings the tale that Virgil invented a magic glass that could be used to see for fifty kilometres. His credulity shows how real and false knowledge rubbed shoulders at the time, for Bacon himself was a genuine pioneer of optics, doing much of the groundwork for the invention of spectacles. Ironically, later writers told the same story about him, asserting that he had devised a telescope with a range of all of eighty kilometres.

Bacon himself was a Franciscan friar who became a famous teacher at Oxford. The first European to give instructions for the making of gunpowder, he also proposed the idea of flying machines and of motor-driven ships and carriages. He was a controversial figure whose unorthodox

An engraving of the brilliant scientist Roger Bacon. As a friar and philosopher too, he was a forerunner of the Renaissance man. Also an eager proponent of astrology, he even suggested putting knowledge of the stars to use to counteract the all-conquering Mongols then threatening Europe.

views eventually got him into trouble with the Church. Twice in his life he was banned from teaching. Although Pope Clement IV came to his aid, Bacon was condemned again following the pontiff's death and even sent to prison by his fellow-Franciscans.

As if the real wonders of his career were not enough, legend proceeded to gild the lily by attributing various other magical powers to him after his death in 1292. According to these later stories, Bacon could raise spirits and summon up the dead. He too was said to have created a talking statue, though in his case it took the form of a brazen head and supposedly he was asleep when it finally uttered. In the end, though, Bacon was said to have repented of his search for forbidden knowledge, retreating to a walled-in enclosure inside a church. "Thus," a biographical pamphlet concluded, "was the life and death of that famous Friar, who lived most of his life a Magician, and died a true penitent sinner and an anchorite."

125

Laughter in the Face of Plague

One distinctive feature of medieval story-telling was the vein of social satire that ran through much of it, with kings, convents and commoners all there for the taking – and no work better exemplified the trait than the *Decameron* of Giovanni Boccaccio.

The *Decameron* was written in the mid-fourteenth century at a time when the Black Death was devastating Boccaccio's native Florence. It describes how a group of ten friends fleeing the plague take refuge outside the city and pass the time in telling stories – 100 in all, often funny, sometimes charming and at times bawdy. Through them all runs a streak of satire and a distaste for pomposity that reflects the author's own temperament and his background as one of the first and greatest pre-Renaissance humanists. But the tales, which are mostly drawn from folk traditions, also reveal the deep vein of anti-authoritarianism that helped humanize a profoundly hierarchical society.

The Lovers in the Nunnery

Typical in its apparent anti-clericalism and its real humanity is the story of Isabetta, a beautiful young nun who, after a short while within the convent walls, took a lover. After dark he would sneak into the convent and the two would enjoy each other's company until shortly before dawn. This happy arrangement lasted some time until one night a nun saw him leaving. From that time on she and her companions kept watch, planning to inform the abbess if he was seen again so that the sinners could be caught red-handed.

In time they spotted the man arriving, and hurried to alert the abbess. But, unbeknown to them, she too had a lover – a priest whom she smuggled into her room in a chest – and he happened to be with her at the time. Hearing the excited nuns at her door and fearing they might break into the room, the abbess pulled on her habit as quickly as she could in the dark and rushed out to discover what was the matter.

When she learned of the nun's transgression, she was furious, forgetting her own faults. The guilty pair were exposed, and Isabetta was dragged to the chapter-house to receive her punishment. But, raising her downcast eyes, she saw something that the other nuns had failed to notice. The abbess, in her haste, had mistaken the priest's breeches for her wimple; now she was wearing them on her head, with the braces hanging down by her ears. When she politely pointed this out, the mother superior abruptly changed her tune. She gave a sermon on the universality of human frailty, and from then on Isabetta found that she was free discreetly to go her own way without interference.

The Accidental Cuckold

A similarly generous-minded tale told of a ruler's reaction on finding that his wife had been unwittingly unfaithful. All was revealed when he entered her bedchamber one night, only for her to insist he had only just left. He realized at once that someone must have impersonated him under cover of the dark, and that his wife had been taken in by the imposture.

A wife takes revenge on her jealous husband by smuggling a lover into another room, from a Flemish edition of the *Decameron*, c.1432.

Furious to have been cuckolded, he nonetheless hid his anger from his wife, realizing both that she had been genuinely deceived and that he would only be dishonoured if the truth got out. Instead he went to where the palace servants slept and silently moved from bed to bed, feeling the pulses of the sleepers. It did not take long to find the one whose heart was still pounding from his recent exertions. Even then, though, the king took care not to make a scandal. He contented himself with shearing off the hair on one side of the man's head so that he would know him in the morning.

But the quick-thinking lad, having realized the king's intention, got up and shaved the heads of all his sleeping companions. So the next day, when the ruler came for the guilty man, he could not tell him apart. Yet, once again, he restrained his anger, simply telling all the servants that whoever it was who had done wrong had better not do it again. Only the sinner understood this warning, and he took care to heed the advice. And so he saved himself from punishment; the monarch shielded himself from public ridicule and, more importantly, preserved his guiltless wife's honour.

Till Eulenspiegel the Prankster

Crude and sometimes cruel, the jokes played by a German peasant prankster delighted audiences across Europe in the Middle Ages, and in bowdlerized versions are still popular with children today.

According to legend, there really was a Till Eulenspiegel – the name means "Owlglass" – and he was born, as the stories maintained, in the village of Kneitlingen in the Brunswick region of central Germany. The date of his birth has gone unrecorded, but he is traditionally said to have died in 1350.

If such an individual did in fact exist, many other tales that originally had nothing to do with him must gradually have become linked to his name. For by the time his adventures were first put down in print, sometime around 1500, he was said to have been active all over Germany and beyond. The earliest surviving account of his adventures dates from 1515, and versions in Dutch, English, French and Latin quickly followed. In more recent times, Till Eulenspiegel has not merely become a hero of children's books but also inspired a symphonic sketch by the composer Richard Strauss and an epic poem by the German Nobel prize-winner Gerhart Hauptmann.

In fact the original tales are hardly children's material, being often scatological and occasionally downright obscene. Their appeal lies in watching Till use his wits to triumph over the unwary, deflate the pomposity of authority figures and escape from looming disaster just when the situation seems most desperate.

Till's Wild Childhood

As the chapbooks told the story, adventure and absurdity followed him wherever he went. Even Till's baptism was eventful, for his godmother got so drunk at the celebration that she fell off a bridge on the way home, soaking herself and the baby, whom she happened to be carrying at the time.

The bedraggled Till then had to be bathed to wash off the river mud, and in later life used to joke that he had been baptized three times in a day – in a font, in a stream and in a kettle.

As a boy Till quickly developed a reputation for scrapes and scamps. Even on horseback rides with his father he could hardly refrain from getting into trouble. If he was riding out in front, he would rudely stick out his tongue at passers-by, while when he rode pillion he would pull his pants down and expose his buttocks – an early example of mooning.

Worn out by the complaints about him, the family eventually decided to move to his mother's birthplace, Magdeburg on the Saale. There he quickly drew attention to himself by his skill at tightrope-walking; to his mother's irritation, he would draw crowds of spectators by stretching a rope over the river and crossing from bank to bank. To get her own back, she once cut the rope when he was halfway across, giving him a good ducking to the vast amusement of the onlookers. He got his revenge on them by promising to perform an extraordinary trick that required each individual to lend him his left shoe. Then he flung the whole pile to the ground in a jumbled mass and stood back to enjoy the confusion and fistfights that ensued as each individual scrambled to try and find his missing footwear.

Soon afterwards his father died, leaving the widow to bring up her difficult offspring alone. Till showed no inclination to help out by learning a craft, though occasionally he used his acumen to get food when they went hungry. Once he pretended to be a baker's boy and persuaded a bread-maker in the city of Stassfurt to give him a sackful of loaves, promising that his master would pay for them at an inn across town. The tradesman sent his own apprentice to collect the money, but Till had put the bread in a sack with a hole in it, and when a loaf fell out, he sent his companion back for a replacement. Needless to say, he took off home as soon as the youth was out of sight, and the family had enough to eat for a whole week.

Triumphing With Wit

Till was always good at using his wits – and sometimes his delight in wordplay – to get a free meal, as a later incident at an inn amply demonstrated. Turning up penniless, he asked the landlady how much he could eat there for. She told him that he could eat at the gentleman's table for twenty-four pence, at the guests' table for eighteen pence or at the servants' table for twelve pence. He settled for the gentlemens' table, where he enjoyed a hearty meal. When he had finished, the woman asked for her twenty-four pennies. He feigned astonishment. Far from paying her, he wanted the twenty-four pence he had agreed to eat for, pointing out that he was a poor man who could not afford to do something for nothing. "As it is," he went on, "I've eaten and eaten until the sweat's pouring off me. I couldn't eat more if my life depended on it. So just give me the money you promised." Fortunately for him, the landlady had a sense of humour and agreed to let him off without paying.

The antics of Till Eulenspiegel made him into something of a national jester in Germany, as he travelled about on his adventures. Such irreverent figures were important in most European countries, helping to bring down the powerful a notch or two. This relief from Innsbruck shows the Habsburg Emperor Maximilian I, flanked by his councillor on the one side and a court jester on the other, c.1500.

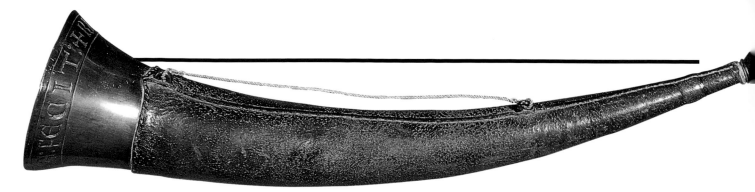

In the best medieval satirical tradition, the stories of Till did not shy away from poking fun at kings and nobles. As a guard at the Count of Anhalt's castle he blew his bugle at all the wrong times – and, in doing so, showed his master up as a fool. This leather-covered copper horn is from Lombardy, *c.*1252.

Adventures Far and Wide

Food was always important to Till, as he showed when he got a job as a guard at the Count of Anhalt's castle. Since his employer neglected to feed him, he in turn forgot to blow his bugle when raiders stole the count's cattle. "Why aren't you sounding the alarm for the enemy?" the count demanded apoplectically when he realized what was happening. "There's no need," Till replied laconically, "the fields are full of them already."

To compound the offence, he blew a false warning just when dinner was being served, sending the count and all his men dashing for their weapons. They returned to find their watchman wiping his mouth contentedly, having finished off the choicest morsels. He quickly found himself looking for a new job.

Eventually his reputation as a trickster spread so widely that he was invited to the Danish court. The king himself offered to recompense his travelling expenses by having his horse shod and, when Till specifically asked, agreed that he could have the best shoes available. So Till went to a nearby goldsmith and ordered gold horseshoes with silver nails. His Majesty good-humouredly paid up when Till pointed out that he had only taken him at his word; in fact, the monarch even offered him a permanent post as court jester.

Having mingled with royalty, it only remained for Till to visit the pope, which he duly determined to do. He ended up staying in Rome at an inn run by a wealthy lady, who laughed at his presumption when he boasted that he would be meeting the pontiff in person. She pointed out that in all her life as a citizen of Rome she had never exchanged a word with His Holiness. Self-assured as ever, Till insisted that he could arrange an audience for her if only she would pay him 100 ducats for the privilege.

When the landlady agreed, he hurried to St Peter's to attend Mass, forcing his way to the front of the crowd. But as he was approaching the Communion rail to take the sacrament, he ostentatiously stopped and turned his back on the altar, holding up the proceedings. His behaviour was odd enough to attract the attention of the pope himself, who wondered if he had a dangerous heretic on his hands. So the pontiff had Till apprehended by guards and questioned about his beliefs. Till maintained that his views were at one with those of his Roman landlady.

This was enough to convince the pontiff to summon the lady herself. She had no difficulty in showing herself to be a good Christian, and in so doing got the personal audience she had long desired. As for Till, he simply echoed everything she said; and when pressed about his behaviour at Mass, he explained that he had held back only because, as a very great sinner, he felt unworthy to approach the altar before making confession – which he had now had a chance to do. Pleased with his answer, the pope let him go – and he promptly claimed his 100 ducats reward.

Eventually Till's riotous lifestyle caught up with him, and he finally fell ill at Molln, near Hamburg. There he was taken to a hospital called the Holy Ghost; he did not miss the irony that, having long prayed for the Holy Ghost to enter him, he had ended up inside it instead. There, in the presence of his long-suffering mother, he died; and a grave claimed since at least the sixteenth century to be his can still be seen in the town.

The Pied Piper of Hameln

Another, much darker, tale of the pomposity of authority also comes from provincial Germany. Known today as a children's story, the tale of a ratcatcher's revenge may have its roots in a real-life tragedy.

On 26 June 1284 a strange figure attired in multi-coloured costume approached the town fathers of Hameln in the Brunswick region and offered to solve a problem that had been troubling them: a plague of rats that infested their larders and cellars. They agreed on terms, and he proceeded to play his pipe from street to street, charming the vermin into following the music. Then he led the rodents to the nearby River Weser, where they all drowned.

The council was delighted to be rid of the pests, but not so eager to pay the bill. The mysterious musician ended up cheated. So sometime later he returned to the town to take a terrible revenge.

Once more he played his pipe, only this time to a different tune. Now it was the town's children that pursued him, all the way to a hill called Koppen. And there they and their leader disappeared, apparently into its slopes, never to be seen again.

Though no contemporary record of the event exists, the legend was so firmly entrenched in Hameln by the late Middle Ages that councillors dated documents "from the year of the transmigration of the children" and banned musicians from the street where the piper had passed. Today scholars suggest that some actual incident may have become confused in the folk memory with a genuine migration out of Saxony to Hungary, or even with the Children's Crusade of 1212. Then, thousands of children from the Rhine Valley set out on a hopeless mission to liberate the Holy Land; most starved to death or were sold into slavery and, like the children of Hameln, never came home.

FANTASTIC CREATURES

Medieval people were fascinated by accounts of bizarre and unfamiliar animals. One stimulus came from travellers' tales, particularly after the crusades sent thousands of voyagers to unfamiliar lands. From classical literature came descriptions of fabulous creatures like the sphinx and the phoenix. A third source was the Bible, and particularly the Book of Revelations, with its descriptions of monstrous beasts prophesied to appear on Earth in the run-up to the Apocalypse. The allure of the subect fed through into heraldry and literature, stimulating the creation of a new artistic genre in the form of the bestiaries (see page 115).

Left: A tournament shield decorated with the arms of the Villani family, from Florence, Italy, 15th century. Symbolic animals were central to heraldic imagery, with lions and eagles prominent choices. The griffin, combining elements of both, was also popular. Known to legend since the days of ancient Assyria and Persia, it served in medieval times to symbolize vigilance.

Below: The seven-headed dragon of the Book of Revelations receives the homage of the worldly in a scene from the *Apocalypse of Angers*, a series of tapestries by Nicholas Bataille (1363–1400). Behind it stands a second beast, described in the Bible as like a leopard but with the feet of a bear and lions' muzzles. St John, the book's author, watches on the right.

Left: Daniel's vision of four prophetic beasts and God enthroned, from an illustrated copy of the commentary on the Apocalypse composed by the Asturian monk Beatus of Liebana, *c.*1100. In the Biblical description, one beast was "like a lion, with an eagle's wings"; another resembled a bear; the third a leopard, but with four heads and the wings of a fowl; and the last was "dreadful and terrible, and exceeding strong", with ten horns.

Below: This elaborately decorated letter "B" (introducing the Latin *Beatus Vir*, or "Blessed is the man") shows the psalmist David as a shepherd rescuing sheep from a bear and wrestling with a lion. From the Winchester Bible, England, 1150–80.

Left: Illustration of a camel from an early 13th-century bestiary. Reports of the animals reached the West via crusaders returning from the Holy Land. Exaggerated in the telling, such descriptions only added to scholars' confusion, for they seemed quite as fantastic as literary accounts of the monsters of antiquity, yet were vouched for by eyewitnesses as true.

THE LEGACY OF MEDIEVAL MYTH

Despite centuries of scientific discovery and industrial advance, the influence of medieval culture on contemporary society remains indelible. And it is not only European institutions which bear its hallmarks. For through religion and art, film and fiction, the myths of the Middle Ages continue to impress themselves upon the modern mind around the globe.

The medieval *chansons de geste* had an immediate impact on the literature of the sixteenth and seventeenth centuries. From Boiardo, Ariosto and Torquato Tasso in Italy to Robert Garnier in France and Lope de Vega Carpio in Spain, the tales of medieval heroes lived on in a wide variety of artistic forms. In England the poet Edmund Spenser and, more famously still, the playwright William Shakespeare both drew on stories from the medieval canon. But one of the most intriguing works of all came from the writer Miguel de Cervantes Saavedra. His novel *Don Quixote de la Mancha* was produced in two parts in 1605 and 1615 – and it rapidly became acknowledged as one of the greatest of all Spanish novels. It tells of Alonso Quijano, a country gentleman so immersed in the world of the chivalric romances he has read that he recreates his life in their image: he is knighted by an innkeeper, takes the name Don Quixote de la Mancha and – accompanied by a peasant, Sancho Panza, as his squire – rides out on a crazy chivalric quest in which he mistakes windmills for giants and sheep for soldiers. The book is generally interpreted as a satire on the romances that Don Quixote renounces at the end of his adventure.

A Taste for Romance

Medieval romance also in time spawned the Gothic novel, a sensationalist genre whose colourful narratives and picturesque settings gave readers respite from the eighteenth century's culture of rationality. Horace Walpole's *The Castle of Otranto*, published in 1764, is often heralded as the first of its kind. Walpole at first did not put his name to this tale of giants, dungeons, terror and supernatural mystery, preferring instead to encourage the pretence that it had been written some time in the eleventh to thirteenth centuries by an Italian

For the Holy Week celebrations in the city of Seville in Andalusia, southern Spain, the *nazarenos* wear costumes and follow traditions handed down from medieval times.

churchman named Onuphrio Muralto. Other significant Gothic novelists included Ann Radcliffe, whose books *A Sicilian Romance* (1790) and *The Mysteries of Udolpho* (1794) were widely read and imitated in Europe, and the aristocrat William Beckford who wrote *Vathek, an Arabian Tale*.

A taste for the exotic and transcendental was also a feature of the artistic movement known today as Romanticism. Its writers, artists and musicians (including Percy Bysshe Shelley, Caspar David Friedrich and Hector Berlioz) stressed the value of subjective emotion, experience and the imagination in revolt against the prevailing reliance on the reasoning intellect. The most self-consciously medieval influence, however, was the revival in architecture of the Gothic style. This not only made a significant impact on the estates of aristocrats, but also on many European towns and cities. One celebrated result is London's Houses of Parliament, designed by Charles Barry and Augustus Pugin and opened in stages from 1847.

The vogue for medieval influences spread right across Europe. In France the Romantic poet, playwright and novelist Victor Hugo drew deeply on medieval epics to produce historical romances including *Notre Dame de Paris* (*The Hunchback of Notre Dame*, 1831). In Britain the Scottish poet and novelist Walter Scott, another great admirer of medieval romances, won the acclaim of a wide public for his narrative verse and historical novels including *Ivanhoe* (1819), which has roles both for Richard the Lionheart and Robin Hood, and *The Talisman*, (1825), about Richard the Lionheart's heroics on the Third Crusade.

Meanwhile, in Germany writers drew inspiration from the twelfth-century courtly love tradition of *Minnesang* ("Love Song") that had flourished under the patronage of the Hohenstaufen emperor Frederick Barbarossa. In 1848 the German Romantic composer Richard Wagner made the first musical sketches for his celebrated opera cycle *Der Ring des Nibelungen*, inspired by the medieval German epic the *Nibelugenlied*. Wagner had already written his opera *Lohengrin*, derived from the story of the Swan Knight (see page 72).

The pre-Raphaelites revived the style of the Middle Ages. This allegory of reconciliation after the Wars of the Roses, by Henry Payne (1868–1940), hangs in the British Houses of Parliament.

The Medieval Example

The year 1848 also saw the establishment in London of the Pre-Raphaelite Brotherhood of poets and artists including Dante Gabriel Rossetti, Holman Hunt and John Everett Millais, who dedicated themselves to recapturing what they saw as the simplicity and purity of vision in late medieval Italian painting during the era before Raphael (1483–1520). They chose medieval subjects and styles in their work, which set itself against the prevailing nineteenth-century aesthetic and provoked controversy and even ridicule – but was championed by the art critic John Ruskin.

The Brotherhood had a short life but a wide and enduring influence. When one of its followers, the artist, poet, designer and craftsman William Morris, founded his own manufacturing firm with Rossetti and other pre-Raphaelites in 1861, his inspiration was the medieval guilds of craftsmen who once executed their own artistic designs; he felt that the old practice offered a positive contrast

135

Robin Hood has proved a staple of late 20th-century cinema. One of the best-known screen adaptations, however, remains Errol Flynn's 1938 appearance in *The Adventures of Robin Hood*.

to what he saw as the ugly mass production of his day. Morris's firm sold hand-made furniture, wallpaper, stained glass and tapestries, reinterpreting much of the work from the Middle Ages. Through the Arts and Crafts Movement, medieval influences reached a new generation.

A Global Appeal

The attraction of the medieval age did not diminish in the twentieth century. A thousand years after the fact, popular narrative in some parts of the world continued to celebrate the exploits of Charlemagne and his paladins. In rural Brazil, Charlemagne ballads are still performed; they are known as *literatura de la corda* ("string literature") because the pamphlets in which they are published are displayed on strings in the marketplace.

Traditional *romancero* ballads are also still known in parts of Spain, Portugal and Latin America where descendants of Spanish and Portuguese settlers live. In Sicily travelling performers lay on puppet shows known as *opera di pupi* in town squares, performing tales from the Charlemagne cycle. The hero of the *opera di pupi* cycle is not Orlando but Rinaldo (Ranaldo), who is often presented as an outlaw and in the homeland of the Mafia is popularly known as the "*mafioso*".

Outlaw on the Screen

One of the most popular figures to have survived from the medieval period, however, is undoubtedly Robin Hood. From the fifteenth through to the seventeenth century, village-green plays and games featuring the forest outlaw were a popular part of English May Day festivities, and stories and rhymes about Robin Hood were a common subject for chapbooks – the small booklets peddled by itinerant merchants at markets and fairs across England from the early seventeenth century on.

In 1795 English critic Joseph Ritson made a collection of the enduringly popular Robin Hood ballads and poems, thus ensuring the character's survival into another era. And by the twentieth century a whole new art form appeared ready to breathe new life into this enduring character.

Robin Hood graced the screen as early as 1922, in the form of Douglas Fairbanks, and the outlaw has since been played by Errol Flynn (1938), Sean Connery (*Robin and Marian*, 1976), Patrick Bergin (*Robin Hood*, 1990) and Kevin Costner (*Robin Hood: Prince of Thieves*, 1991). There have also been many television adaptations, comic books and a Disney cartoon version (1973), not to forget a spoof film directed by American Mel Brooks, *Robin Hood – Men in Tights* (1993).

The heroic themes of medieval legend proved irresistible to Hollywood, which found in these ancient tales the same rich source of love and drama that had entertained people centuries before. They also provided an excuse for lavish sets and costumes. The 1950s and '60s saw a glut of historical epics inspired by the age of chivalry. They included *King Richard and the Crusaders*, based on Scott's *The Talisman*, in 1954; the 1961 hit *El Cid* inspired by the saga of Don Rodrigo Diaz de Vivar and starring Charlton Heston in the title role with Sophia Loren as his wife; and *The Lion in Winter*, a British success of 1968.

Swords and Sorcery

In recent years, medieval themes have found a new popular outlet in fantasy. The novels of British academics C.S. Lewis and J.R.R. Tolkein, published mainly in the 1950s, drew inspiration from the tradition of chivalry and epic. They won a vast audience and gave birth to a whole new genre of literature which still thrives today. Lewis, a specialist in medieval romances, began a series of seven children's novels, the Narnia Chronicles, with *The Lion, the Witch and the Wardrobe* in 1950. They featured the adventures of English schoolchildren in a parallel universe, Narnia, accessed initially through the back of a wardrobe in an English country house; the children fought the forces of wicked enchantment with the aid of a Christ-like lion named Aslan. Tolkein, a specialist in Anglo-Saxon and Middle English literature, wrote *The Hobbit* in 1937 and the three-volume *The Lord of the Rings* in 1954–55; the second an epic quest narrative featuring a diminutive hero, the gnome-like Frodo Baggins, who with the help of a wizard named Gandalf has to keep a venerable and powerful ring from the grasp of evil forces by delivering it to its destruction by fire in the belly of a distant mountain.

The books had enormous influence, especially *The Lord of the Rings* which sold eight million copies globally. They helped to spawn an international industry producing comics, board games, video games and thick fantasy books centred on quests conducted by fearless heroes and heroines, helped or hindered by sorcerers, in a bigger, brighter world derived ultimately from that of the medieval romances and epics. A film version of *The Lord of the Rings*, scheduled to be made in three parts and directed by Peter Jackson, went into production in New Zealand in autumn 1999.

The medieval period in Europe continues to inspire performers, artists, film-makers and writers, and to fascinate historians. Its popular legends have spread like a many-branched river through the intervening centuries, and still give life to remarkably diverse areas of global culture as the third millennium begins.

In View of Camelot, by Rodney Matthews, one of the world's most popular fantasy artists. His work has appeared on posters, album covers and in numerous books.

Glossary

aquamanile A kind of vessel used to hold water with which to wash hands at table or during the Mass.

chansons d'amour The songs of courtly love (*amour courtois*), derived from Provencal troubadour poetry, which gave rise to the development of the courtly romance genre of literature.

chansons de geste The "songs of great deeds", a name given to the genre of literature which dealt with epic tales of heroes such as Charlemagne.

ciborium A vessel used to hold the Host for the service of Holy Communion.

fals' amors A term of courtly love meaning, "false love", used to denote an unworthy recipient of a knight's love.

fin' amors The courtly-love term for "true love", the aim of all chivalric knights.

hejira The Arabic term used to describe Mohammed's flight to Medina. Means literally, a "breaking of ties".

jihad Literally "holy war", an Islamic concept which believes that the soul is at war with the forces of darkness on behalf of Allah. Interpreted by some as a similar concept to the Christians' crusade.

La Reconquista The term used to describe the crusading zeal of Spain's Christian rulers during the reconquest of the various territories held by Moorish Islamic rulers.

lai A type of narrative poem usually concerned with tales of courtly love. The most celebrated exponent of this genre was the twelfth-century woman known as Marie de France.

Matamoros The name given to St James of Compostela, which means literally "killer of the Moors". In this guise he was used as an image of *La Reconquista*.

merce A term from the lexicon of courtly love meaning "pity", the emotion a woman should show to her suitor after he has demonstrated his "worth" by enacting heroic deeds in her name.

psalter A book containing the psalms and often a liturgical calendar, litany of the saints and various prayers.

reliquary A shrine for keeping or exhibiting a sacred object or relic.

scutage A system introduced in feudal times enabling landowners to express their allegiance to the king in terms of a cash payment rather than the more burdensome personal service.

sharqiyin An Arabic word for Easterners, the term from which the English word "Saracen" is derived.

sotie Short, secular play performed in France at carnival time to poke fun at human foolishness.

taifa "Party kings", used derisively to denote the squabbling of the leaders who allowed Moorish power in Spain to fragment into competing power blocs.

valor An attribute of the successful chivalric knight, suggesting "courage".

Index

Page numbers in *italic* denote captions. Where there is a textual reference to the topic on the same page as a caption, italics have not been used.

139

Further Reading

Broughton, Bradford. *Dictionary of Medieval Knighthood and Chivalry People Places and Events*. Greenwood Press: New York, 1988.

Cobby, Elizabeth. (ed.) *The Pilgrimage of Charlemagne*. Garland: New York, 1988.

Coffin, Tristram P. *The Female Hero in Folklore*. Seabury: New York, 1975.

Evans, J. (ed.) *The Flowering of the Middle Ages*. Thames and Hudson: London, 1998.

Farrier, Susan. *The Medieval Charlemagne Legend: An Annotated Bibliography*. Garland: New York, 1982.

Frayling, Christopher. *Strange Landscape*. Penguin: London, 1995.

Hamilton, R. and Perry, J. *The Poem of the Cid*. Penguin: London, 1984

Holmes, George. (ed.) *The Oxford Illustrated History of Medieval Europe*. OUP: Oxford, 1988.

Keen, M. *A History of Medieval Europe*. Routledge and Kegan Paul: London 1967.

Keen, M. *Chivalry*. Yale University Press: Connecticut, 1984.

Keen, M. *The Outlaws of Medieval Legend*. Routledge and Kegan Paul: London.

Kightly, Charles. *Folk Heroes of Britain*. Thames and Hudson: London, 1982.

Knight, Stephen. *Robin Hood the Outlaw*. Blackwell: Oxford, 1996.

Loomis, R.S. and Loomis, L.H. (eds.) *Medieval Romances*. The Modern Library: New York, 1957.

Own, D.D.R. *Eleanor of Aquitaine: Queen and Legend*, Blackwell: Oxford, 1993.

Saul, Nigel. *Age of Chivalry: Art and Society in Late Medieval England*. Collins and Brown: London, 1992.

Swan and Hopper. (eds.) *Gesta Romanorum*. Dover Publications, Inc.: New York, 1959.

Picture Credits

The publisher would like to thank the following people, museums and photographic libraries for permission to reproduce their material. Every care has been taken to trace copyright holders. However, if we have omitted anyone we apologize and will, if informed, make corrections in any future edition.

t top; **c** centre; **b** bottom; **l** left; **r** right

AA&A	Ancient Art & Architecture, London	DBP	Duncan Baird Publishers, London
BAL	Bridgeman Art Library, London/New York	ET	e.t. archive, London
BL	British Library, London	RHPL	Robert Harding Picture Library, London
BM	British Museum, London	V&A	Victoria & Albert Museum, London

Cover BAL/BL; **title page** ET/BL; **contents page** ET/Archaeological Museum, Friuli; **6** Tony Stone Images, London/John Freeman; **7** BAL/Sixt Parish Church, Haute-Savoie; **8–9** ET/San Vitale, Ravenna; **10** BAL/Musee Conde, Chantilly; **11** V&A; **12** BAL/V&A; **14** BAL/Bibliotheque Nationale, Paris; **15** ET/Louvre, Paris; **16–17** Tony Stone Images, London/Oliver Benn; **18** AKG/Bibliotheque Nationale, Paris; **19** BAL/Kunsthistorisches Museum, Vienna; **20** AKG/Israel Museum, Jerusalem; **21** ET/Church of the Martorana, Sicily; **21** BAL/Louvre, Paris; **22–23** ET/Bibliotheque Nationale, Paris; **24** BAL/Musee Conde, Chantilly; **25** AKG/Bibliotheque Royale, Brussels; **26** BAL/BL; **27** AKG/National Library, Vienna; **28t** V&A; **28bl** BAL/Accademia, Florence; **28br** ET/Bibliotheque Nationale, Paris; **29t** Sonia Halliday Photographs, Aylesbury; **29b** V&A; **30t** Sonia Halliday Photographs, Aylesbury/Bibliotheque Nationale, Paris; **30–31** RHPL/Robert Frerck; **31l** ET/Louvre, Paris; **31r** RHPL/Duncan Maxwell; **32** BAL/Private Collection; **33** Glasgow Museums/ The Burrell Collection; **34** ET/Biblioteca Marciana, Venice; **35** RHPL; **36** BAL/Musee Conde, Chantilly; **37** BM; **39** AKG/Bibliotheque Nationale, Paris; **40** BAL/Stapleton Collection; **41** BAL/Kremsmunster Abbey, Austria; **42** BAL/BL; **44–45** BAL/BL; **46** V&A; **48** Oronoz, Madrid; **49** Oronoz, Madrid; **50** BAL/Museo Arqueologico Nacional, Madrid; **52–53** Institut Amatller d'Art Hispanic, Barcelona; **54** AA&A; **55** RHPL/K. Gillham; **56** BAL/The Barber Institute of Fine Arts, University of Birmingham; **58** BAL/Bibliotheque Royale de Belgique, Brussels; **60** BM; **61** AA&A; **62** AKG/National Museum of Ireland, Dublin; **63** BAL/National Gallery, London; **64** BAL/BL; **65** V&A; **67** BAL/Musee National du Moyen Age et Thermes de Cluny, Paris; **68** BAL/Bibliotheque Nationale, Paris; **69** BM; **70–71** AKG/ Bibliotheque Nationale, Paris; **73** BAL/Louvre, Paris; **74** BAL/BL; **75** AKG/Notre Dame de Fontevraud, Fontevraud; **77** BAL/BL; **78** ET/Medieval Museum, Rome; **79** RHPL; **80** BAL/Louvre, Paris; **81** BAL/Bibliotheque de L'Arsenal, Paris; **84** AKG/BM; **85** BAL/ Musee National du Moyen Age et Thermes de Cluny, Paris; **86** Corbis, London; **88t** ET; **88l** Bodleian Library, Oxford (MS 186.7f.313v); **88–89** V&A; **89** BAL/BL; **90** The Stockmarket, London; **91** AA&A; **92–93** Michael Holford, London; **94** Bibliotheque de Dijon; **96** St Nicholas' Hospital, Harbledown, on loan to the Canterbury Heritage Museum; **97** BAL/Bibliotheque Nationale, Paris; **98** The Master and Fellows of Corpus Christi College, Cambridge; **100** ET/Museo del Duomo, Friuli; **101** Mick Sharp Photography, Caernarvon; **102–103** BAL/Bibliotheque Nationale, Paris; **104** ET/Lisbon Museum, Lisbon; **105** RHPL/Charles Bowman; **106** Jean Williamson/Mick Sharp Photography, Caernarvon; **107** BAL/BL; **108** The Board of Trustees of the Royal Armouries, Leeds; **110t** ET/Bargello, Florence; **110b** Tony Stone Images, London/Gary John Norman; **110–111** BL/DBP; **111tl** BAL/Musee Conde, Chantilly; **111tr** V&A; **112** By kind permission of the Dean and Chapter of York; **113** ET; **114** Jean-Loup Charmet, Paris; **115** BAL/Bibliotheque Nationale, Paris; **116** JCD Smith, Somerset; **118** ET/Real Collegiata, San Isidoro, Leon; **119** Corbis, London; **120** Corbis, London; **121** ET/Bibliotheque Nationale, Paris; **122** BAL/Musee Conde, Chantilly; **124** BL; **125** ET; **126–127** ET/Bibliotheque de L'Arsenal, Paris; **129** Tiroler Landesmuseum Ferdinandium, Innsbruck; **130** Arthur J. Page/Faversham Town Hall; **132t** V&A; **132b** BAL/Musee des Tapisseries, Angers; **133tl** BAL/ BL; **133bl** BAL/Fitzwilliam Museum, Cambridge; **133r** BAL; **134** Axiom, London/Alan Williams; **135** BAL/Houses of Parliament, London; **136** Warner Brothers/Ronald Grant Archive, London; **137** Rodney Matthews/Usborne Publishing, London.